"Great read and I truly enjoyed it. Allowed me to see my mistakes and how to correct them. It's a hard truth that we must nurture our kids to what their potential and desires are not what we want them to be. The genius in Tri-C Parenting is in its simplicity. As parents we struggle to develop confident and productive young adults who are ready to go out into the world and find their passion. Dr. Rees gives us the tool to do just that. Tri-C Parenting should be the go to manual every parent should possess. Simply enlightening! "

- Ingrid Kohlmorgen, MD OB-GYN

"Parenting is hard…..Dr. Rees' highly informed approach to this crowded space is very welcome. Rather than providing lists of strategies and techniques, Dr. Rees helps the reader to understand fundamental and foundational concepts that will inform thoughtful parenting… (he) uses humor, gentle confrontation, and frank logic to help parents recognize past errors and future directions for improvement. I will enthusiastically recommend Tri-C Parenting to my patients!"

-Beth Lusby, PhD Child, Adolescent, and Adult Neuropsychologist

Principal, Cornerstone Assessment and Guidance Center, LLC

"I loved the book. There were times that I actually laughed out loud….It was an easy read, and the application of the Tri-C strategies seem achievable. I appreciated the straightforward calling out of bad parenting choices, but then giving parents a framework for changing first their behavior and then their children's behavior…I would absolutely recommend it to friends and clients."

-Lisa Y. Pierce, MD Child and Adolescent Psychiatrist

"A great read! …Dr. Rees has always impressed me with his easy rapport and insightful acumen… I am happy his book has finally come to fruition so that it can help guide a broader population of parents who may be struggling with their children's behaviors."

-William T. Goldman, MD, DABPN Child, Adolescent, and Adult Psychiatrist

**Tri-C
Parenting**
Clear • Confident • Complete

Follow the Formula

Brian Rees, PhD

Tri-C Parenting: Clear. Confident. Complete.

I have changed some names to protect individuals' privacy.
This book does not replace the advice of a medical professional. Consult your physician or licensed therapist before making any changes to your regular mental health plan.

Copyright © 2024 Brian C. Rees

All rights reserved. No part of this book may be reproduced or used in any manner without the prior written permission of the copyright owner, except for the use of brief quotations in a book review.
To request permissions, contact the publisher at reescore@gmail.com.

Paperback ISBN: 978-1-7367584-3-4 (3rd Edition)
eBook ISBN: 978-1-7367584-4-1
Library of Congress LCCN: 2024907730

First Paperback Edition: April 2024

Tri-C logo design by: Monique Hayes
Cover art by: Keny McClurg

Published by Rees Core Inc.
400 N. Main St. Ste. 104, Grapevine, TX 76051

www.TriCParenting.com

Tri-C Parenting: Clear. Confident. Complete.

"Learn it. Know it. Live it."

— Brad Hamilton

Brian Rees, PhD

CONTENTS

Introduction 3

Let Me Set the Table 6

You and the Relationship 14

Clear 57

Confident 127

Complete 152

References 170

About The Author 172

Brian Rees, PhD

Tri-C Parenting: Clear. Confident. Complete.

Introduction

You are reading a new version. The first release was a soft launch—this is the grand opening. My initial book was published in late 2021, and after a year of gathering feedback from readers, I wanted to update the original and better explain how to implement the Tri-C system. I spent most of 2023 adding to and heavily revising the entire thing, and hopefully created exactly what you need. Here it is.

Hello, parent! My name is Brian Rees, I'm a child/adolescent/family therapist, and a dad of three. Welcome to the land of legitimacy. I've been a full-throttle, massively busy mental health professional in private practice for more than a decade and a half. I've treated thousands of kids and helped all types of parents. Trust me, I've seen and heard it all.

Here's the good news: You, the parent, are the number one agent of outcome in your child's life, more than any teacher, coach, or friend. Mighty powerful words. You have volunteered to enter a special realm of great responsibility—a position that can feel just as wonderful as it can feel like too much.

And here's why I wrote this book: I'm done with all the family decay and bad parenting and internet-generated garbage and shootings and other senseless things like that. Everything does start at home; a pivotal setting that is designed personally by the parent(s). Kids raised right don't become spoiled children, neglected juveniles, robotic pawns of their parents, or overly submerge themselves into the mind-numbing digital world—they become good people with the ability to forge their own healthy paths and create positive, fulfilling lives.

I feel the need to put my hard-earned experience out in the world. The moment it dawned on me was a few years ago, at a seminar, and one of the featured speakers melodramatically stated, "There is no parenting script."

My first thought was: *Um, yes there is.* Then I wondered why I had immediately gone to that in my head; it certainly felt right. I realized it was because I'd already effectively coached all kinds of parents on just about every challenge imaginable. Regardless of what their child was like, I utilized (with tremendous success) the fundamental parenting blueprint that I'd personally crafted. I also realized I'd been asked by people throughout my professional career, "Do you have a book? Or something online? You make it sound so easy."

So here I am with a formally developed approach that can work for nearly any family. No matter what type of person you are, what type of kid you have, or what the world happens to be like, think of Tri-C as a primer to assist you in this glorious adventure. Because the last thing you need is "just another parenting book." *Yawn.*

My guess is that you're reading this for one or two reasons: You are experiencing some troubling issues with your child, and/or you would like some professional guidance in today's ever-changing society of, well... an exhausting list of hurdles. We keep hearing that the mental health crisis in our youth continues to rise as society continues to cultivate difficulties young people aren't equipped to manage. By themselves. Hopefully Tri-C can help us parents fix that.

So know this: Whether kids are six or sixteen years old, most haven't been on the planet long enough to have developed significant issues. By themselves. But various degrees of dysfunction appear to be present in our younger generation, and the main reason is that we parents—who possess such tremendous influence—aren't sure how to equip ourselves to effectively navigate all the parenting duties we are tasked with. And as the world continues to move forward, we're charged with more and more family challenges.

I understand why that seminar presenter wants you to believe there is no parenting script. After all, humans (parents and children) vary significantly. We come from a mixed treasure chest of backgrounds, deal with diverse social norms, and range in skill sets and personal experiences. As individuals, we possess contrasting personalities and belief systems, and communicate and interpret information in a variety of ways.

But we adults all desire the same outcome—to be responsible parents who raise great kids—and a sound formula consistently produces the desired results because there's hardly any variation. The objective is to raise your new, original person successfully (i.e., not to become a replica of you, because there already is a you), and to do that we must minimize variation, stay rooted in reality, and become the best parental version of ourselves to shape the best possible version of our child. There is a way—the Tri-C Way—and it starts with you.

Ask yourself this: What if there was a relatable approach to successful parenting, *real parenting*, created by a professional, that's conveyed in a way that nearly every parent or parental figure can grasp and implement? A valid guidebook, so to speak. That would be awesome, right? There is, and I'm going to show you.

Let Me Set the Table

Nothing is perfect, but I've worked to get this parenting system extraordinarily close. Year after year, it continues to prove true. Maybe I'm too ambitious, but what I'm really trying to accomplish is end about 98% of the difficulty of normal parenting. What I mean by "normal" is that both parent and child are reasonable people who can act mature enough and develop healthy interpersonal relationships. Unfortunately, there are some humans who simply cannot.

The gloomy reality is we have adults who are not coachable when it comes to parenting. They're too self-centered, lazy, painfully hard-headed, or who welcome drama and chaos for whatever reason. I'm not going to indulge those individuals, so we'll eliminate all the nonsense. You deserve authenticity and honesty, and that's what you're going to get.

The concept of great parenting is not as confusing as many people want or make it out to be, just like the concept of staying physically healthy, regardless of body type, centers around only two things: regular exercise and clean eating. It's the steady application that makes it so incredibly hard, which is why I assume we're constantly bombarded with new-fangled work out/diet plans.

Although we've got a few more elements in the mix, it's essentially the same hurdle for good parenting: **commitment**. But a nice difference is, the better of a parent you are, the "better" humans your children become. In other words, over time, your kids will visibly prosper and make child-raising easier (I don't know about you, but staying on a good diet and working out ALL THE TIME never seems to get much easier.)

I'll teach you how to interact effectively, allowing you to fully enjoy being a parent as you raise your kids constructively. Once you learn from this philosophy what children ultimately need and how to provide it, it's more about consistency than anything else. So clear your head, settle in, and get ready to absorb this super valuable information.

Tri-C: Clear • Confident • Complete

Clear: "Why can't you act like an adult!"
"Uhh, I'm only twelve?"
We have to look at our children through a clear, objective lens because they are not grown-ups. Half the time they don't know what they're doing, so we can't expect them to act like it. When we have unrealistic expectations for someone (anyone), we get frustrated and disappointed, which is terrible. When we demonstrate frustration and disappointment towards our children, it damages the relationship, and that is bad, bad, bad.

Tri-C says you cannot parent successfully unless you have a positive relationship. This is the highest ranking factor of good parenting, so get ready for lots of relationship building material. The more your kids like you, the more they'll be inclined to do what you say.

Confident: Steady, genuine confidence can be elusive; however, it's the game-changer for humans. Life is designed to be hard for everyone, but self-confident people enjoy it more than all others. The world we live in is a challenging place, which means we must relentlessly empower our children to strive and believe in themselves. We chose to have kids, and life is now about them because they need us more than we need us. They are prepped and ready for anything, and how we directly parent them will either lift them up or take them down. If life can be defined as a series of experiences, then our experience as parents is arguably the most important one we'll ever have.

Complete: Tri-C is a complete parenting process, and our kids need us to be totally invested throughout their entire upbringing. Completing essential parenting tasks every day, every month, and every year might sound daunting (which includes quite a bit of sacrifice), but it gets much easier when we commit to Tri-C. However, if you think "easier" means shirking your responsibilities or cutting back on your commitment, think again.

Disclaimer: Tri-C is designed to work for everyone and can be implemented at any time, unless your child:
- Is moderately to severely autistic or struggles significantly with a cognitive processing disorder
- Has a sub-80 IQ
- Was gravely abused or neglected in some capacity
- Has a personality disorder (or a parent with a personality disorder)
- Is battling a pronounced drug or alcohol problem
- Is suffering from pervasive anxiety or a depressive disorder
- Has a parent at war with the other

NOTE: All these require professional treatment.

Here are some aspects that make my approach different than nearly all the other hundreds of parenting strategies/books out there. Aside from the fact that Tri-C *actually works*, I'm not going to attempt to dazzle you with a bunch of psychobabble, long-winded personal stories, entertaining make-believe narratives with stressed out teen characters and frustrated/confused parents, unnecessary statistics, graphs, and charts. You'll find none of that here. That excessiveness causes most readers to get overloaded and lost. Nor is this regimen based on selling you a feckless, trendy-sounding catch phrase technique that's designed to hook you and trick you into thinking *Aha! If I just do that, then all of my parenting problems will be solved!*

Tri-C is a fundamental formal application. This book is meant to be read front-to-back and I've kept it brief because there's no need for you to be swamped with too much information. I know you're busy and you've probably got lots of things going on, so I want you to easily flip back through to reread sections as you see fit, or be open to rereading the entire thing until you get it. And let me add—because this is where your level of desire to be an awesome parent comes into play—for most of us it takes a strong willingness to "get it," especially when it pertains to understanding and executing something so weighty.

To get good at something (and I mean good) consists of executing fundamental principles. Let me give you an example. If you've ever been taught how to swing a golf club the right way...*wow!* It feels super funky at first, and much like certain aspects of parenting, it's different than how you would naturally want to do it.

Needless to say, there are basic steps involved. Step one: *Here's how to hold your hands.* Step two: *Here's how to place your feet.* *Step* three: *Keep your head down and pull the club straight back, etc., etc.* To just play a friendly game of golf, we don't necessarily have to learn the proper way to swing a club, but if we want to play golf well, there's a right way to do it. If we want to play serious golf, we must first master the fundamentals.

The same goes for becoming an amazing artist, or an outstanding musician. Oh sure, most of us can paint a picture, pluck a guitar, or hack away at golf, but to become accomplished, we must first commit to the core components. Once the fundamentals are in place, the golfer, artist, and guitar player can then develop highly advanced skills and take their pursuit to a whole new level. Just ask any professional coach or instructor—they preach the fundamentals then constantly reinforce them as needed.

Great parenting is no different. I'll do my best to teach you the root elements, then use my professional experience to help take your parenting prowess to the upper echelon. But to make all of this work, you must commit to executing the basics and faithfully stick to the program, no matter what might be happening at any given time with you or your children.

Let me reemphasize this: consistency is the name of the game. There are times we all can act lovely with our kids. But children are very impressionable, and every time we treat them negatively, cave in, or stop being a parent, it leaves a mark, and some of those wounds can be deep. Too many blemishes and successful parenting cannot be achieved, just like too many bad shots on a golf scorecard equals failure. Nor can we allow any harmful aspects of parenting to become normalized. If you're already on that path, let's get you off.

The parents in my office are often scared and frustrated because their kids are too defiant, seem unusually odd or oblivious, have ADHD, dabble with drugs/vapes/alcohol, or feel depressed or anxious. Effectively raising children is hard enough, and when you throw in one or more of these problems—combined with worn-out parents—things can go downhill fast.

I developed this parenting philosophy to work in the most challenging parent-child scenarios because I had to. You'll read a lot about difficult situations (some of you will identify with, some of you not so much), but I also have plenty of valuable information for families who seem to hum along peacefully—Tri-C is strategically forged to be applicable for all of today's kids. If things are going relatively well, it's most likely because you are a marvelous parent or have responsible-acting children who are genetically programmed to be cooperative and not grappling with any personal issues.

Of course, some of you might be marvelous parents, but you've got a kid who is taxing to deal with and hard-wired with an inflexible mindset (possibly paired with an emotional or learning problem, which can enhance difficulties). We do not get to determine how our child is manufactured.

Yep. Hard-wiring. We're intrinsically hard-wired in lots of different ways, like being either right- or left-handed, artistic, fast or slow, or brilliant or not so brilliant. Those characteristics are not decided by us, although most human traits can be enhanced over time with hard work. To elaborate, children **do not choose** to begin their lives acting out or having personal difficulties. Why would they? Why would these little humans who essentially have no power deliberately welcome any problem from their parents or society and make life that much harder? **It is important that you understand this.**

I will emphasize this issue throughout the book because it's a fallacy that must be overcome. The "clear lens" of Tri-C teaches parents to focus on helping their kids grow up gainfully and improve instead of obsessing about their shortcomings, regardless of what those might be.

So let me go ahead and start that campaign right now. Parents who legitimately fancy themselves normal: If your child is confusingly difficult or clearly struggling with something, that human *did not choose* to be engineered in a way that would foster problems. My professional assumption is the kid is genetically predisposed to struggle with certain aspects of functioning, and is continuing to respond poorly to an incorrect parenting approach. As you can imagine, my office is filled with these families.

Parents who have not been formally taught how to best deal with a child who is having notable issues are going to experience recurring challenges. Therefore, Tri-C is configured to teach caregivers how to interact constructively, create a connected relationship, and to successfully advance their young person, no matter how the kid has been primarily assembled. Tri-C won't make home life perfect because people aren't perfect, but it will make things abundantly better.

Unfortunately, there are misguided parents who make everything worse, becoming so chronically frustrated that it causes the suffering youngster to have a terrible experience growing up. That dark childhood road leads to feeling negative about oneself, which is unacceptable and can ultimately create a pitiful existence. This is the exact opposite of what we want, especially when it doesn't have to be that way.

What I'm saying is, for lots of frustrated, ornery, discombobulated, rambunctious, or disengaged kids (which certainly does not mean they're bad kids), "acting out" or "acting wrong" can become a regular thing. However, life tends to upgrade tremendously, and behavior improves when the parents learn how to create the Tri-C home environment.

But sometimes, a sound Tri-C baseline has been established for a few months and serious problems continue. In that case, odds are the kiddo is stricken with something formidable (e.g., major depression, mild autistic traits or ADHD symptoms intensely heightening, anxiety causing negative coping mechanisms, regular drug use) and help from outside the home needs to be considered. The first choice would be to locate a top-tier mental health professional who treats young people, but if that's not a viable option, then some type of formal assistance or program in the community operated by devoted adults. Consult your pediatrician and school counselor about what they think and have them meet with your child. These professionals often have knowledge and access to resources that you don't.

I encourage everyone to firmly maintain Tri-C even when you seek other forms of help. The basic principles of this timeless model are for all families. No matter who you are or where you live, success will come if these fundamentals are carried out religiously. I know some of you might be thinking this does sound too good to be true, but as mentioned earlier, I've been at this for a long time and chances are your kid isn't a unicorn. So, get ready, get set, and let's move forward with a proven and complete way to parent. All kids deserve it.

You and the Relationship

A very good buddy of mine was chatting with me about some teens who had been over for his daughter's 15th birthday. He said he knew most of them, and he knew what some of their parents were like.

He shook his head, "Dude. I know we've talked about how important good parenting is, but as I stood back and observed, I never realized it until I was watching some of these kids. The ones who acted mature and nice, you know—respectful—have awesome folks. But the ones I knew who have lousy parents were a whole different story. What a difference."

Not getting to meet you and talk to your child creates some hurdles, but I'll do my best within these pages to teach you this approach. I've also learned over the years that most of you can pull this off, but some of you won't. I hate to admit it, but it's true. If you're successful with Tri-C it's because you were able to put aside your frustration, anxiety, and excuses. You will have allowed yourself to recalibrate your thinking and welcomed how to execute this culture of parenting.

Tri-C is mostly about showing you how to change, which in turn will motivate your child to be more receptive to you. Whether we like it or not, the heavy lifting is on the parent because, as the adult, you have all-encompassing power in this arrangement. If a parent wants to have a high-quality kid, the caregiver has to be fully devoted to making some adjustments and become a high-quality parent—there's no way around it. If you're not in the business of being a super solid parent and make this a five-star priority, then stop reading.

I know we've got some young parents out there who are still working on their own maturity and development, when at times it can seem extremely overwhelming to develop another human. If Tri-C is implemented correctly, child-raising becomes tremendously easier for all parents, regardless of their age. *Execute these fundamentals. Follow the formula.*

I don't believe I can accurately express Tri-C with a bunch of sugarcoating, and there's nothing sexy about great parenting. Because this is an instruction manual (not a J.K. Rowling fantasy or Dan Brown thriller), you might not find it to be wildly exciting reading material (nor am I anywhere close to being able to write like those two literary wizards—no pun intended *Harry P.*), but hopefully, it's potent enough to keep your attention. I understand that placing a powerful emphasis on mastering the fundamentals of nearly any undertaking can feel monotonous, but again, I'm not trying to impress you; I'm here to educate.

Most of the parents who come to my office tell me they appreciate my straightforward manner. You've probably noticed I'll use that same approach here. I'll write these words as if we've already developed some trust and you're cool with me speaking very candidly. Getting to sit across from someone is great because there's a back-and-forth interaction created and specific questions answered, but no worries; you and I will do our best.

And because these printed words are all I've got, some of you might feel like I'm occasionally being a bit brash or trying to call you out. Please understand that I'm not attempting to offend anyone—I'm trying to drive home an important point. Parts of what you read may not feel very comfortable, but I've also realized that if I pull punches, certain parents' ability to understand and administer this strategy will be minimized. Some of you will be changing your parenting persona and pushing a hard reset. That's a good thing.

Something else to note, you're going to see some repetition. Why? To rewire certain hardened areas of the brain **is not easy**. Most people believe what they want to believe and think they *need* things to be a certain way (sadly, we all are guilty of this) and in this case, how children are supposed to behave. I've had super sharp parents return to my office like it's Groundhog Day because we have to revisit some of these principles (which is totally fine), but some of them feel obligated to apologize. No apologies are needed; it can take some time to sink in!

So when you find I'm repeating myself regarding various concepts, know that it's on purpose. There also are no throw away lines; everything you read is deliberate. I've also had many sessions in my office with parents who are at their wits end, fearing that nothing will work to make things better. But as these meetings progress and they are able to calm down and *listen* to what I'm saying (which is often something I'd expressed earlier), I can see their faces soften and their eyes light up with hope.

And once the dedicated adults get it—just like when things "click" for fully committed athletes—it's wonderful. I also encourage spouses and significant others to consider reading this book together, especially during the first encounters of implementing Tri-C, to help coach each other and to passionately stay with it as it begins to work.

Obviously, the more invested in the kid, the better; therefore, allow me to consistently motivate you to A) fully obtain the correct mindset and B) employ the basics. Because those two whopping principles mostly constitute the fabric of Tri-C, they will show up frequently throughout the book. I must do everything possible to make sure you can devour and realistically carry out these convictions, especially when your kid is acting disagreeable in some fashion or you're worn thin. Again, to learn the bedrock of good parenting isn't especially riveting but totally necessary. Just keep absorbing and we'll get to the more engaging stuff later—some groundwork has to come first. In this chapter, I'll cover some general, fundamental Tri-C features, then we'll get to the nitty gritty starting in chapter three.

So let's get going and take a look at the stunning, current version of you! In a classic system developed by Diana Baumrind, parenting styles can roughly be categorized as Permissive, Authoritarian, Neglectful, and Authoritative. Some of you may have seen this before; however, I've added one called "Compassionate Boss" because I encounter an impressive amount of these folks in my office. Let's determine your tendencies as you should fall into one of these categories.

Permissive. You're more of a friend than of a parent. You certainly love and want the best for your child, but you tend to enable. You hesitate to enforce age-appropriate rules, easily cave, tolerate inappropriate behavior and/or disrespect, make up excuses, and dislike conflict. Example: You allow too much time playing video games to avoid potential confrontation and because you want your child to "be happy." You do not rock. Not yet.

Authoritarian. You are in charge! You love and want the best for your kid, but you yell and harshly punish for not meeting your requirements. You are always right. You provide direction *ad nauseam*, deeply enforce your own personal agenda, never apologize, and communicate however you want. The authoritarian tends to disregard the mighty value of the parent-child union, and it's "Do it my way or else!" You sound super fun.

Neglectful. Uninvolved. Disconnected. Selfish. Immature. This negligent, excuse-making bum of a parent provides little support if any, and rarely reads parenting books.

Authoritative. Vastly different than Authoritarian, although you are the captain. You love, respect, and prize your child to no end. You set age-appropriate, reasonable rules. You empower and do not enable. Your consequences and rewards are fair and consistent. You teach self-responsibility and avoid lectures. You strongly honor the parent-child relationship, encourage cooperation, act mature/composed but still have fun, maintain relatability, and instill confidence and the emotional support necessary for your kid to create healthy goals. You rock.

Compassionate Boss. You demonstrate many of the same positive characteristics as Authoritative, although you tend to communicate in a more straightforward, demanding style as you blend in a little Authoritarian force. Easygoing kids can mostly tolerate this approach because they see the big picture and understand your abruptness is wrapped in goodness and love. However, strong-willed children are more black-and-white thinkers. They often fail to see the big picture, want what they want, wrestle with change, and struggle to read between the lines (i.e., they often misinterpret meanings and regularly take things too personally). Therefore, a compassionate boss–willful child combo can routinely experience problems. You somewhat rock, but keep reading.

Authoritative sounds best, and my guess is most of you want to parent this way or intermittently try to parent this way but somehow get derailed. I am a realist, so I understand I cannot change your personality, nor do I want to, and I think it's fantastic that you're taking your valuable time to read this. But if you fall more into the Permissive, Authoritarian, or Compassionate Boss types, you will be asked to permanently adjust some of the ways you interact with your kid. Again, Tri-C is about what works, and to make things better, everything has to start with you know who.

As you begin to administer this practice, it can be uncomfortable to alter an old, locked-in parenting style that might sometimes work or worked when your child was younger. You're reading this book because you possess a strong desire to better understand your kid and to be a great parent, and in the deep crevasses of your mind, especially when your old habits are screaming at you to return to your prior, unproductive ways (because you're a human), you know you must devote yourself to a new method.

Lesson One: Respect

Everyone hates feeling disrespected. Everyone. A foolproof way to not like somebody is for that person to treat you with disrespect. That should do the trick. So how about we scrutinize what arguably is the *numero uno* trademark that sabotages respectfulness in a parent-child relationship, then work on fixing it.

This common flaw is based on a classic yet detrimental adult belief that states we know how our kid is supposed to act, and how we parents should get to act. Although some parents adhere to it more strongly than others, as the authority figure(s) in the parent-child arrangement, the age-old doctrine goes something like this:

I'm the adult; you're the child. I can say whatever I want and treat you however I want, and I should expect you to meet all reasonable expectations.

Of the three parts of this notion, the first and last parts are accurate.
I am the adult; you are the child.
Correct.
I expect you to meet all reasonable expectations.
Correct.
However, there's a twist concerning the middle section: *I can say whatever I want and treat you however I want.*

Hold up.

When our child is choosing not to meet an expectation (e.g., "Get off your phone." "Quit sneaking food in your bedroom." "Stop hitting your brother!") and we become frustrated, it's easy to get worked up and communicate abrasively. Sometimes we seem to discount that our child is a real person, and we treat that young human with zero consideration (another thing we are all guilty of). Permanently fixing this negative behavior is extremely difficult, but has to happen. That is why I have placed "staying respectful" as the first big issue to address. You might be thinking: *Of all the parenting topics he could've opened with, he chose this.*

Yes, I did.

Regardless of whether we're the parent, stepparent, single parent, foster parent, or family member raising the kid(s), we have:

<u>Two Primary Parental Tasks</u>

1. Appropriately protect our children.

2. Appropriately develop our children.

Everything falls under these two cardinal umbrellas. Therefore, we must communicate in a certain style so our kids will trust us, like us, and do what we say. Our children must mind us so we can keep them safe, and *want* to listen to us so we can prepare them to become high-functioning adults. We have to earn credibility with our kids. (Yes, I said we have to earn it—not demand it. We don't get to decide how other people feel, including our children.) If we can't communicate effectively and our kids do not embrace our guidance, then we fail to meet the two primary tasks, and good parenting goes out the window.

Why can parents act so ugly to their child—the entity they cherish above all things in the galaxy? Because we are people. And when our kid isn't listening, being disagreeable, making a dumb decision, or maybe we're just having a bad day, we can get emotionally charged and fall into the habit of believing: *Because you are my child, I can say whatever I want and treat you however I want.* That's what we call arrogant and disrespectful, and I'm assuming you're not normally an arrogant or disrespectful acting person.

When I earlier stated that some of you will be able to carry out Tri-C and some of you will not, a major factor will be your ability to consistently interact respectfully. Again, that's why I launched with it. Tri-C mandates that the parent must treat the children with constant respect, regardless of the situation. *("Regardless?"* I can hear you asking.) This is difficult to commit to but a very learnable practice that comes with a huge payoff. Don't worry! As you continue reading you will see how all this falls into place, and without turning you into your kids' doormat, Tri-C helps you become the relatable parent in charge and who is part of the solution, not part of the problem. When the adult ultimately honors laziness or arrogance, the children become innocent victims instead of transforming into the most impressive versions of themselves.

Here's an example: A frustrated mom and her somewhat headstrong (yet likable) adolescent son were in my office getting into it. Although her actions were understandable, I thought, *Uh oh, this lady is blowing it.* Her harmful approach completely derailed the goal of productively discussing why he was doing badly in two of his classes.

As soon as he felt defensive and got a little surly toward her, her parental tone negatively shifted. Downhill they went. Instead of choosing to take just a second and acknowledge her child's naturally iron-headed personality (which, remember, he did not ask for), she quickly did what many parents would do: She gave in to anger and grabbed the "gas can." *Ka-boom! Argument explosion!*

Constructive conversation over. Credibility deterioration. She allowed her frustration to dominate her thinking and behavior. *I'm the parent! Do not argue with me!*

The mom and I, of course, kept working together, and once she learned to automatically activate Tri-C guidelines in these types of scenarios, no more explosions occurred. I mean it. Because their relationship had gotten behind the eight-ball, she, being the adult, was responsible for luring him back to a place of positivity. And eventually, she did. Victory! No more hyped frustration; no more fighting; no more back-and-forth disrespect.

The young child who had grown into a teenager finally trusted his mom again, and was much more receptive to fulfilling his responsibilities. (Whoopie!) She abandoned her old, destructive thinking: *You are my kid; just do what I say!* and embraced a new, correct mindset. She committed to putting in the work, and her kid naturally followed.

1. She officially trained herself to accept the fact that her son wasn't hardwired to see the big picture and be easily agreeable. Sort of a bummer, but still okay; very workable.

2. She stopped herself from getting emotionally provoked by him. (This is a toughie, and maybe the most difficult fundamental step to conquering.)

3. She discovered a way to interact with him in a way that actually works.

Why do some parents give up on Tri-C? Because it's hard. *At first.* Being around people (especially the same people) day after day can be grueling, particularly when it's a kid—your kid—who might be acting difficult and causing you to want to return to being forceful because *I'm the parent!*

I mentioned earlier that children tend to naturally be either more cooperative or more rigid-minded. Let me add that this personality characteristic is on a continuum, just like being either more introverted or extroverted. (Note: What I mean by continuum is all humans fall somewhere along this unit of measurement.)

On one end of the scale there are essentially trouble-free kids who are hard-wired to be compliant and emotionally mature. They "get it." On the other end are more problematic kids who are wired to be single-minded and emotionally immature. They don't "get it." For many of us parents, our kids' genetic disposition tends to influence how we treat them. Hence, children who are more innately mulish make it hard for us to keep our cool and stay respectful.

Dr. James Dobson, the author of the highly touted book, *The Strong-Willed Child,* warns that parenting an inflexible kid can lead us to become a screamer and/or a tyrant, as that young person constantly pushes back and can make it painfully challenging to find the balance between love and control. I had a frustrated dad in my office discussing his oldest son. He asked, "Do you treat any strong-willed kids?" My first thought was, *If I had a nickel…*

But I smiled and answered, "If I see 45 kids a week, 25 are in here because they're strong-willed."

He replied, "Then I've come to the right place. My kid seems to act defiant just to be defiant. When I tell him to do something, he'll actually cop an attitude and ask me why. Can you believe that?"

"What do you say?" I asked.

He huffed, "'Because I said so!' That's what I say."

I winced a little. "And how does that go?"

"Well, lately, pretty badly." He paused. "Now that I'm thinking about it, I don't think that kid can stand me."

I appreciated this father having enough awareness to see that his child didn't like him, and regrettably, why would he? This dad certainly had likable traits, but every day he acted more and more like a jerk as he tried to force respect. That never works.

Now listen, some of you may think, *My kid has to respect me—I'm the parent*. Let's address that mental misconception right now, because if we're going to get real, then no, your child does not have to feel respect for you.

Here's more insight regarding genetics and personality. For emotionally mature children, negative interactions with their folks are minimal because empathic, open-minded kids understand it's in their best interest to act respectfully. They're in the business of keeping the peace, not flipping over the apple cart. We can pretty much parent them however we want. They may not like us if we continually act forcefully or disapprovingly, but they will mind us. They have the ability to see the big picture and placate nearly any type of adult.

However, humans are not automatons. That is why a fair amount of this manual addresses how to parent children who do not automatically want to mind, and as mentioned earlier, don't "get it." As soon as we become frustrated with them, many of these kids get defensive instead of capitulating. As a matter of fact, I'm not sure there would be any parenting books past the toddler years if all kids mechanically minded their parents. I'm not kidding.

That said, some parents must raise intrinsically hard-headed children who play from a "stubborn" deck of cards, and many of these new humans show up on Planet Earth. They tend to have tunnel vision, and getting what they want (or being right or having the last word) is the most important thing to them, making parents bonkers. Because these types of kids can be short on empathy (placing value on others' wants and feelings, especially if it doesn't align with *their* wants), big problems with their folks regularly emerge. Baffled parents in my office of these types of children will ask, "Wait a minute, you mean my kid was born like this?"

I'll nod, "That is correct."

Unfortunately, a willful kid and frustrated parent can become at serious odds as the child actually loses "obligated" respect for the overly commanding adult. The agitated child will regularly begin to defy, manipulate, lie, argue, and try to fight with or wear down the caregiver—either passively or aggressively—to determine what the frazzled parent will allow because why the heck not? "I don't like you, and you make my life worse anyway, and I don't want to recognize that if I stopped provoking you and acted more agreeably, you would be nicer to me." If this becomes the culture of the parent-child relationship, guess what happens? Down, down, down you go (*where it stops, nobody knows*).

Believe it or not, your child knows who's the big cheese. If you have a stubborn kid (ranging anywhere from mild to severe on the obstinate scale), who evolves into not liking you? *Crash and burn.* The relationship will grow into a "me versus you" dynamic, which is awful. Regrettably, I assume a decent number of you readers can somewhat identify with this, and you did not intend for your role as a parent to unravel like that. If this sounds familiar, whether you've got a strong-willed kid or not, know this book is designed to teach you an assortment of fundamental concepts, including how to satisfy these two important questions:

1. Can I, the adult in the driver's seat, maintain a high level of overall maturity and awareness when dealing with my kid, anywhere and in any capacity? In other words, can I get past my self-importance, keep my cool/dignity, and faithfully foster a positive family lifestyle?

2. Can I, the adult, consistently use an effective method of communication so that my child will *want* to comply with my parenting year after year, anywhere and in any capacity? In other words, can I interact constructively and unfailingly honor the relationship?

Again, what I'm trying to convey is that successful parenting starts with the powerful adult, not the kid. Your child was born with inherent personality traits, and that's just how it is. Orchestrated properly, Tri-C dictates the **parent** can adapt to whichever type of person the kid is, and the **parent** can interact in such a way that the kiddo will consistently be motivated to follow the adult's guidance.

Here's an illustration involving a parent who had not bought into effectively advancing her child. Some of you probably have witnessed this parental ridiculousness before. I saw a hardened mom at Six Flags screaming at her eight- or nine-year-old son who was behaving like a spirited pony with lots of energy.

"What's wrong with you!" she screeched. (Meanwhile, I'm thinking, *What's wrong with you?*) "You need to listen to me! Get over here!" She grabbed him by the arm and got in his face with a few more choice words as he scowled and tried to pull away. We have a decent idea of that mom's twisted thinking:

1. I'm in charge. I can treat you with zero respect, especially if you've upset or scared me in some way.

2. How dare you continue to defy me! You make me treat you like this!

3. Everyone witnessing this needs to know I'm powerful and in control, and the best way to show that is to be fearsome!

What in the world was she trying to accomplish? Where was she going with that?

I've had self-willed children in my office break down and cry because they feel tremendous internal conflict as they struggle to be more aware/mature/cooperative, but they aren't yet developed enough to mitigate those personality features. As mentioned earlier, this is the most common issue I treat: kids who tend to be hardheaded and don't know how to handle various life challenges, including how to get along with their parents. Navigating childhood and adolescence is hard enough for young people these days, even the ones who mostly comprehend what is happening around them.

For inherently stubborn kids, their parent's job is to recognize that particular hardwiring and not to make things worse. Trust me, lots of parents become slaves to their frustration and make things worse. These people must train themselves to do the opposite and make things better. How? By being the champions who help productively advance these "tough-to-raise" individuals into pleasant—yet—strong adults with high self-confidence, determination, and a decent sense of consideration for others. *Hello, Tri-C.*

Maintaining a positive relationship with children like this takes extra work, as many of these unnerved parents report spending all their time trying to deal with their kids' oblivion, which gets exhausting. And this "oblivion" can evolve into all kinds of negative personal and social issues as adolescents become adults, which is why it is so important to interact with them properly while they're still our responsibility.

And, not uncommonly, parents with an innately hard-headed child can get tricked. Their kid can have beautiful, random moments of total clarity. Unlike Forrest Gump, who reminded us at every turn that he had "issues," parents of a willful child often think, *My kid does get it! I can actually relax and communicate however I want!* Don't get caught up in that fantasy.

You're a human, and your child is a human, and human beings "want what they want" and generally have the means to acquire it. That's why we rule the planet. You are an adult who has learned that if what you desire is not what the establishment allows, you will suffer a consequence if you resist or get caught doing it. Regardless of *your* natural degree of willfulness, through years of experience, you've made the proper adjustments.

Children do not have that luxury. They are not experienced people but still powerful entities: naturally moody, feeling overruled, yet vigorously testing the world around them. This is very normal. (You wouldn't believe how many parents I've talked with who never lied to their folks, snuck out, cheated on a test, or smoked marijuana/drank underage. Astounding). Keep this in mind when you're being challenged to any degree, as most parents fall into the trap of getting angry too easily, giving up, being hypocritical, or taking what their kids say or do personally.

Many parents, mostly moms, get caught up in allowing their child to make them upset or hurt their feelings. Mothers, unfortunately, tend to be regarded as readily available, soft targets who are more vulnerable to being manipulated or wounded.

Therefore, with some kids, the "age-old doctrine" flips. "My mom isn't scary and will love me no matter what, so I can treat her however I want!"

When humans feel emotionally hurt, we tend to respond negatively. Although all of us parents are (ahem) mature, we are still people who are sometimes completely drained, impatient, and vexed by disrespect: all parent-child relationship wrecking balls.

Well, guess what? A child or teenager is just a goofy kid who doesn't need to possess any emotional power to provoke you when it comes to hurting your feelings or making you upset.

You can stay reserved and not blow up.

We will revisit this concept throughout the book because it's such a parenting handicap and must be overcome. **Harsh, knee-jerk responses triggered by our anger/fear/hurt are bad and immediately throw a wrench in the entire process before we can even begin!** Strictly speaking, when your child is being defiant or clueless or sassy, do not take that kid seriously. I will help you train your brain in this department, and we will vigorously address this rule of Tri-C because I cannot emphasize it enough.

You may be thinking: *Wait a second. It can be upsetting and it's never acceptable for my child to be disrespectful to me to any degree.* I totally concur. However, when it does happen, Tri-C teaches you a mindset to instantaneously fall into where it won't upset you, and a communication approach to apply where your kid will no longer feel inclined to be that way. This is a critical, opening feature of the process: switching from interpersonal to transactional.

As parents, *we know* when we're responding harshly or inconsiderately to our kid, so moving forward, now is the time to recognize that and stop rationalizing our negative actions. In other words, we parents are charged with starting a new trend of interaction with our child.

I've also treated too many kids who complain that their parents generally don't seem to care who they are, what they think, or how they feel, which is sad to hear. They tell me they feel they're in some kind of bleak simulation as their folks treat them with zero courtesy, act put out, or lecture and bark orders all the time. More fortunate adolescents tell me they feel encouraged because their parents treat them with dignity. They see how some other parents negatively interface with their kids, and they greatly appreciate the continuous efforts their own parents' model to stay understanding.

In other words, they know their parents have the discretion to communicate however they want, but because their engaging folks choose to act respectfully, it heavily motivates them to return the respect. They get it. They see it. They are positively influenced by it, and from time to time when the situation calls for it, they'll refreshingly comment, "Thanks for being such a great parent!"

> Know this: A child will follow a parent's lead because you are the leader. You set the tone in the household and that is a fact: either more upbeat, connected, composed, and respectful, or more negative, threatening, inconsistent, or disconnected.

Now, back to the frustrated dad in my office. Once this loving yet distressed father could accept the hard fact that he had an innately temperamental child, he realized he would need to be the one to change instead of expecting his kid to supernaturally change. He was able to shift his focus to what was more important. Rather than hopelessly clutch the perspective of: "I'm the parent! You will do what I say!" he finally came to understand this:

The most important thing is for my child to be receptive to my parenting. This is on me, not him. I've got to adjust because I'm the adult here and he's just a kid. I must alter my predetermined mindset and learn an effective communication method. Because if I don't, then what? He won't ever learn from me all the things I'm supposed to teach him. Will we fight constantly? Catastrophic!

Again, a large part of the first "C" of the Tri-C Model, *clear* expectations, promotes respectful dialogue. When we consistently act civil (regardless of the situation or how we're feeling), it motivates our young human to act civil, and allows us parents to better give our attention to preserving the relationship instead of giving in to reactionary selfishness, adult entitlement, and negative thoughts toward our very own (or adopted) flesh and blood. Feeling negative about our own child stinks and is unacceptable.

I've seen numerous parents who've become so disenchanted with their kid, most of their interactions have become horrid and any remnants of good parenting are gone. Their ongoing anger or resentment towards their child prompts them to hastily throw kerosene on the flame (or just give up) instead of utilizing their power to fix things. It's tragic.

Allow me to restate an important truth that will help you stay respectful, even when your kid is acting mouthy or irresponsible. Everyone knows who is in charge: *You. The parent.*

You are in charge because you have to be, and you possess the ability to make your kid's life wonderful or dreadful; all parties know this. You have all the authority, and your child has none. It doesn't matter if your human is three-years-old, twelve-years-old, or seventeen-years-old, you do not have to argue in any fashion, nor question who has the power.

The only power a kid has is the amount of power the parent has allowed.

Try your hardest not to get overly upset when your kid chooses to be disagreeable in some way. There are plenty of ways. Every time we respond negatively, we poison our parenting and take three steps back.

Poison my parenting? Three steps back? From what?

To reiterate, as parents, we have to persuade our kids to like and respect us. Please burn this concept into your brain. We must continuously build our case year after year for our children to want to do as we say—not have to do what we say. There is a huge difference, and you know what I mean. Our kids cannot afford for us to get lazy, discouraged, disconnected, or consistently frustrated or we will lose them. And they unquestionably need us, especially in today's crazy world.

Raising a human is the most valuable endeavor you will ever engage in. As you commit to the long game of parenting, when it's done right, it's a *selfless game*. You've been personally tasked to develop another person to become healthy on the inside and out, and get to adulthood feeling as self-assured as possible. Indeed—this is a great responsibility.

If you were in my office and I figured you parented either more dictatorially or dismissively, we probably would explore that and try to understand why you felt the need to be that way because that won't work. And during this conversation, if you were open to embracing what Tri-C is all about, my hopeful assumption would be that you are willing to dedicate yourself to doing what needs to be done to become an extraordinary caregiver for your kid. I will not mislead you and advertise that first-class parenting is a walk in the park, but I will reinforce that the Tri-C system, implemented faithfully, makes parenting exponentially easier and more joyful, which in turn, also creates more free time and happiness for you. You win and your kid wins! But as we know, winning at most things requires serious effort.

Throughout this book, I will stress learning how to be aware of how you're interacting with your child, no matter the circumstance and no matter the kid's personality, and choose to engage the right way—the Tri-C way—because it is *worth it*. Tri-C helps the parent to stop enabling, disengaging, or caving in. It helps to stop communicating forcefully or acting unhinged, and expecting the kid to brainlessly follow the parent's direction. I'll show you how to steadily interact correctly so your young human will consistently accept your parenting and thrive from meeting your direction.

Sometimes adults seem to forget their child is not some puppet to move around however they see fit—the kid is a real person, the most invaluable investment ever, and a direct representation of the parents, whose outcome is indisputably shaped by the caregivers' 18-year management style.

You are the sculptor. Your child is the clay. Your interaction shapes that clay, and it's your clay to shape. (Or Play-Doh, whichever metaphor you like.) Do not think for one second that Tri-C is about me asking you to wear kid gloves or boxing gloves. It's a respectful, clinically-based system that epitomizes effective parenting, period.

Lesson Two: Relationship Design; Directive vs. Connected

Lesson Two focuses on the most powerful, fundamental dimension of productive parenting: the formation and continuation of the parent-child relationship. *Okay Brian, I've heard that before, but what is considered a great relationship with my kid?*

I'll explain, but let me first reference an earlier analogy. Some people might naturally be exceptional at "playing the guitar," while others may not. Regarding people skills and the ability to consistently relate to our kids, we don't have to possess "Eddie Van Halen-level" talent to develop warm bonds with our children and constructively raise them.

What I'm saying is Tri-C is a formula—*a robust formula*—designed for nearly any type of parent to follow. This relationship doctrine cannot be dismissed in any fashion:

1. **A positive relationship is the cornerstone of successful parenting.**

2. **A negative relationship will be the mighty downfall.**

These two truths are in bold for a reason. If our relationship with someone is good (and we all desire healthy human connections), we're motivated to maintain it because we like the person and want to be liked in return. But what about our feelings and behavior toward someone we do not like? That looks much different. We don't care what that person wants or how the person feels—and it doesn't matter who we're talking about.

Although we wear a few different hats with our children, we essentially are the boss. During our own working careers, most of us have had a good boss and a bad boss. The good boss you genuinely like! You're not necessarily going out after work, but because of how graciously you're treated, you honor that person with the utmost respect, especially when you know that individual doesn't have to treat you considerately. You're much more open to working hard and meeting demands.

But the bad boss who acts disrespectfully, critically, and/or dismissively towards you creates an entirely different response. You honestly can't stand that bozo and DO NOT CARE what that jerk wants, and the only reason you act dutifully is that you need a paycheck. Yuck. Whether you like it or not, you will create a version of one of these two approaches at home. Your kid will either feel more positively or negatively towards you. (*I'll take positive, thank you very much.*)

There are two different ways to style the relationship. First up, the Directive Way (*boo*). Parents like this mainly focus their attention on behavior, i.e., what the child is or isn't doing. They place unfair conditions on their kid, and erratically demonstrate love, respect, and approval.

These parents tend to hyper-focus on how they personally think things should go or how they're personally feeling, not on executing a productive parenting approach for their kid's well-being. They make most things about themselves, feeling the child should adjust and be okay with however they want to communicate (although they would rarely admit it). When we make things about ourselves, we're not being good parents.

The second method is the Connected Way (*hooray!*). This also involves responding to behavior, but the mature, confident parents consistently demonstrate monumental respect and interest in who the kid is, and put the child's developmental needs first. These dramatically different practices will create two very different brands of relationships.

It's natural for a traditional-minded adult to submerge into and prolong the Directive Way. As a parent, *if I must protect and develop you, I must unduly focus on your actions* (especially at the onset of child-rearing when that little rascal likes to run through the parking lot and sling oatmeal all over the kitchen and whack the TV with a plastic bat). This brings us back to regular demonstrations (especially when we're worn out) of: *I'm the parent; you're my child; do what I say!*

An early custom of significant control becomes the norm. The practice of "do what I tell you" has to work because it's exhausting trying to reason with a three-year-old. But that small child quickly grows into a six-year-old who can be more reasonable and talked with instead of talked at. No one likes to be talked at, by the way. And for that matter, nobody likes to be controlled or told what to do or how to be, and this includes your human child. Being overly controlled will hurl any kid into the "I don't like you" department. Let me rephrase that so I know that you've got it: You don't like being controlled; neither does your child.

If we're being honest, the commanding "just do what I say" approach is an easier way to parent. It alludes to the old philosophy of "I say jump, you say how high." Woefully, this relationship-crushing, disrespectful application is so commonplace and so regularly executed it might be fair to say it's the primary destroyer of effective parenting. (Shame and guilt are also up there in the rankings, and many parents don't even consciously realize when they're manipulating their kids that way. Oh wait. Did I say parents manipulate?)

The worst part: Many parents love feeling powerful—even if it's inappropriately, unnecessarily powerful. I know this sounds terrible, but it's true. It's almost as if they finally have somebody they can boss around and treat however they want. "That's my kid—isn't it my God-given right?" If you haven't already, consider looking into the research project/movie, *The Stanford Prison Experiment*, and you will see what I mean.

When I see parents behave this way, I try to help them take an honest look at themselves and stop that type of interaction because it's causing their kids to actively dislike and disrespect them, which kills what we're trying to accomplish here. These types of parents are honoring their arrogance and/or laziness instead of upholding their responsibility of raising another person successfully. *Their person.* Very sad. And what makes it even more regretful is when we realize the magnitude of this fallacy if it's not positively corrected, and for most families, it's almost always fixable.

Another factor that fuels a disconnected relationship is that grown-ups and children, whether blood or not, do not have much in common. There's a reason adults and kids don't hang out (unless it's family). It's the parents' job to be responsible for the protection and development of their children—not to be their friends (until they graduate from high school). It's almost paradoxical to pull off being friendly without being a friend. Did you catch that? We're not their friends, bros, or besties we share our secrets/troubles with. We're the caregivers for 18 years.

But wait. The most pivotal component of good parenting is *for my children to like and respect me so they will be more responsive to all that I communicate, from how much I love you to eat your green beans to getting high is not permitted.*

Okay, Brian, then what you're expressing is that I must work to find the sweet spot throughout my child's entire upbringing? The sweet spot between managing my kid (which must include control) and consistently demonstrating an unwavering likability/connectedness, even if my child does something bad? Or I'm worn out?

Correct. This is your objective, especially as your child gets older and grows in awareness. As you dedicate yourself to respectful interaction and execute the Tri-C principles, the parenting sweet spot becomes much easier to hit. Why? Because you've put in the profound effort to carry out terrific parenting, your child now responds positively to you. *Bingo.*

This brings us back to the Connected Way: We're clearly as interested in who the child is as in any behavior that's being demonstrated. When parents express constant, meaningful investment, that must certainly indicate how much respect there is for the kid as *a person.* There is no such thing as a healthy interpersonal relationship without trust and respect.

I find myself wanting to say to intimidating parents who like to dominate situations, "Why don't you get off your high horse?" But of course I don't say that. Instead, I'll suggest, "Your child should never fear you—only the consequences you can impose." These misguided folks almost always respond with vapid comments like, "Aw, come on…"

As adults, we must communicate with other adults respectfully; otherwise, we would have zero friends and zero credibility. Therefore, we must maintain this principle when interacting with our children. *The same rules apply. People are people.* I often tell parents, "You're very likable and you know how to get others to like you; get your kids to like you."

Once the Connected relationship is established (after we've learned to get over ourselves) and the young individual knows you're committed, here's what happens: Your child feels accepted by you, the all-important caregiver. That's going to start your child down a developmentally healthy path in life, which differs from the destructive path created by the critical, detached, worn out, or controlling parent. That road leads to doom.

The world is a big, scary place for a child, and your appropriate interaction at every turn gives your kid the reassurance to feel secure, which fosters more "normal" functioning. Normal functioning leads to easier parenting, and I think it's safe to say we are all into easier parenting.

Emotionally deprived or beat-down kids become full of self-doubt and can feel like they don't have much to live for; thus, they can make a lifetime of harmful decisions just to feel better. They'll develop unhealthy coping mechanisms like self-victimization, hurt themselves or others, jockey for inappropriate attention, do drugs, cower, self-sabotage, or demonstrate glaring defiance. On the other hand, children who are richly parented and invested in life feel good about themselves, have a lot to lose, and feel empowered to achieve success. These kids develop healthy ambitions and want to succeed.

They know their parents have the means to upend a desired way of life if bad choices are made.

Plainly stated, the Tri-C fostered Connected Way relationship energizes your kids to want to mind you. *They'll want to.* But this is where your massive dedication to patience, selflessness, and understanding come into play as you create a positive culture of communication. You'll forge an eternal, loving bond due to your fabulousness, and your children will grow in confidence, accept your leadership, seek your approval, and become more inclined to meet real-world expectations. Although there's plenty of room to move around in the sandbox of life, it has rules and parameters—we simply need our kids to learn from us how to navigate them.

The closer you are to your kids, the easier it will be for you to understand how your children communicate and interpret information, which will help you find the correct broadband for transmittal. As the parent, it's our responsibility (not theirs) to match frequencies. *We're the adult with more developed communication skills.* Plus, you'll more easily detect personal struggles throughout their upbringing. Have no doubt: there will be difficulties, and that applies to all young people. None of us are Superman or Wonder Woman.

You'll be trusted, confided in, and able to have open conversations and provide vital support when needed. For example, if legitimate depression has crept into a child's life, the parent must be able to recognize that and appropriately address it. Regarding all childhood issues, we're expected to properly assist our kid and help that young person learn how to figure out life (assist, not rescue or take over). We have the know-how; our kid does not.

Clearly, up to this point, I've primarily talked about you, not your child; we'll discuss some child issues later. As we press on, I again want to emphasize that you have all the power, and your kiddo will respond to you and to life based on how you consistently choose to interact. When you stay in the correct mindset, you will recognize that every delivery regarding every interaction is meaningful, and, when Tri-C is executed regularly, your child (regardless of hard-wiring) benefits! But you must commit to this approach, or as highlighted previously, none of this will work.

Parent-Teen Connection:

"Keep in mind that high school kids—no matter how big the boys, no matter how beautiful the girls—are still mostly children inside."
—Stephen King, from the novel, *Fairy Tale*.

As we know, the parent-child connection tends to change dramatically when little kids grow into older kids—that's why I wanted to include this discussion in the *Relationship* section. Not only can teenagers go back and forth from exhausting to delightful in a heartbeat, but the significant developmental jumps they make throughout adolescence can be difficult for parents to deal with.

This is the time when kids naturally separate themselves from their parents and develop their own identities as they prepare for upcoming independence. Due to this normal phase of uncoupling, these young humans' boundary testing and lack of interest in their folks make it tough to have enjoyable chats with them about personal/recreational things. This leaves us irked and we find ourselves having more of these stiff, administrative discussions that are also known as "lectures."

It's hard to have been so passionately linked with our child for 12 years or so, then suddenly realize *the kid doesn't seem as interested in me anymore*. Try to accept this sporadic developmental truth and vigorously uphold your position by being Connected, not Directive. Also, remember your teenager still knows you're in charge. Don't get tricked. Nothing has changed in the power sphere. You're just dealing with a bigger, smarter, and slightly more mature individual who might try to make you think otherwise.

Regardless of how much or how little time you're spending together, try to stay positive, remember your adolescent is still new to life, and focus conversations on non-administrative subjects at every opportunity. Otherwise, your teenager could perceive you as nothing more than the unrelatable boss and disconnect even more.

Parent:
"Did you do your homework?"

"Did you hang up your clothes?!"

"Why isn't your room clean?!!"

"Why are you always on your phone?!!!"

Blah blah blah blah blah blah blah...

I've heard one parent after another lament the decline of the bond with an aging teen, so understand: the process of reconnecting in adulthood (where the two of you will spend the majority of your time together as two adults—which, I know, sounds crazy) is easier if you evolve appropriately as a parent as your kid evolves as a human being. The more understanding you are during the later child-rearing years, the more credibility you'll have, and the more your teenager will enjoy being around you.

Yes, it's probably easier for dad's to relate to their teenage sons, and yes, the same goes for most moms and their daughters. However, there are still frequencies that match for different genders, it just takes a little more work to locate and maintain them. Which, again, is the responsibility of the parent.

I stated earlier I wouldn't kill you with a bunch of charts/graphs, etc., but I need to at least include this timeless list of developmental tasks of adolescents, composed in 1948 by Robert Havighurst. It's spot-on and great information for you to know:

1. Achieving new and more mature relations with peers of both genders.

2. Achieving a masculine or feminine social role.

3. Accepting one's physique and using the body effectively.

4. Achieving emotional independence of parents and other adults.

5. Preparing for marriage, family life, and a career.

6. Acquiring a set of values and an ethical system as a guide to behavior; developing an ideology.

7. Desiring and achieving socially responsible behavior.

Obviously, the better we are as parents, the easier it is for teens to effectively meet these tasks, especially for kids who struggle to see the big picture, which brings me to this scenario. I was working with a closed-minded, 14-year-old girl and her mom (the apple hadn't fallen far from the tree), and I asked the daughter how much she felt the discussions with her parents were administrative.

She wrinkled her nose and said, "About 80-percent." After her mother stepped out, the adolescent frowned and amended her statement. "It's more like 95-percent."

When I had them switch places, the mother tried to defend herself and puffed: "It's because she won't do what we say." I hear this a lot. That's why this book contains specific ways to teach parents to motivate their kids to consistently meet their requirements and see the value in learning to become responsible.

While we're on the subject of teenagers—because those people are at the age where they mostly know what they should (and should not) be doing—realize that it's beneficial for the parents to do more listening instead talking. You've probably heard this before. *But it's true.* For some of us, this will be another important mental recalibration. A listening approach allows kids the opportunity to work out their own problems, develop healthy coping mechanisms, and put together self-directed answers.

What helps us parents to quit preaching is understanding when we're serving our own anxiety or agenda rather than furthering our child's development. If the kid is shutting down, it's clearly recognizable and indicates that we're not communicating effectively. *Take a breath.* We can either let it go and trust that there will be an opportunity to revisit the topic, or create a two-way street and reshape that monologue into a shared discussion, so the kid will want to listen. As in: *I'll talk. You talk.* Not: *I'll talk, and you sit there and listen to me flap my gums.* When we're lecturing, our kid is not listening, and we're making it about us. It becomes a silly waste of time and energy. Some parents tell me they "just can't help themselves," which I think is a load of you know what.

As parents, we certainly have experienced opinions that we want to convey. I'm saying there are productive ways to express those wise messages. I can't begin to tell you how many parents I've met who continue to lecture even after we've discussed its ineffectiveness. But I've also seen parents train themselves to stop the lectures, place a higher priority on the relationship with their kid than on their own arrogance, and lean into being conversational, which we'll get to shortly. (You may be thinking: *Telling my teenager what to do is being arrogant?* Yes, if you do it all the time and/or get long-winded.)

In the mom-daughter situation described above, Dad came to the session the following week. He was a nice enough guy, but he continued to bang his head against the wall when it came to telling his daughter what the expectations were, rather than recognizing that his communication style wasn't working. (What's that well-known definition of insanity?) He was solely focused on how he wanted his daughter to be, also known as the dreaded Directive Way.

His naive approach demonstrated it was more important to him to just "tell her what to do" rather than mentally reconfigure his parental thinking and consider what was especially critical: to have a great relationship. And because his hard focus was on expressing his opinions and making his daughter meet his requirements, there was no personal connection. She didn't care what he wanted. And why should she other than receiving a punishment?

In the parents' defense, this particular adolescent wasn't very easy to bond with. Aside from being hard-headed and trying to become her own person, she wasn't all that warm and fuzzy, although she was likable enough. Parents tend to align more easily with a child who consistently minds them, and a kid who "gets it" tends to be more naturally affable.

Parents of a more willful child must recognize that and know there will be extra work involved to create and sustain a positive relationship. It takes a lot of understanding and work, as in *I get how you're hard-wired; therefore, I have to keep that in mind and dedicate myself to communicating with you the correct way and not blow it, especially when you're being immature or uncooperative.* Otherwise, there will be no relationship. No relationship means no credibility, and no parental credibility equals defiance and misery. Tri-C is here to help you from being the parent who bangs your head against the wall and who mistakenly thinks that lecturing works.

Thankfully, the parents in the above example kept coming to see me. They realized they had a good kid; she just happened to develop into a teen who would no longer respond to a Directive parenting style. It finally began to dawn on them:

They had to shift.

This was not easy at first, but they obligated themselves to the process and slowly began to recognize that if they wanted their kid to willingly meet their requirements, they would have to become parents who were Connected (loving, aware, mature, and patient), not Directive (frustrated and commanding). They committed to her overall well-being, and it worked. She opened up and became more agreeable because her parents focused on listening to and respecting her. In other words, they focused more on the relationship instead of her actions, which instinctively inspired her to meet the parents' normal expectations. *Ta-da!*

Here's a productive, fundamental example of how to be Connected rather than Directive. Instead of providing an ego-driven, first-hand account to give a life lesson, make a parenting point, or just "tell" the teenager what to do, parents can respectfully explore the best way to effectively address the situation. To eliminate (or at least minimize) these common communication mistakes, a conversation will start rather than a lecture. You'll find most issues can be solved together.

Here's what not to do:

Kid: Man...I don't want to work on my project.
Mom: Which class?
Kid: Biology. Ugh.
Mom: Well, you better go do it.
Kid: Yes, I know.
Mom: Is this the same type of project you did last semester? Here's what I would do: I would get all my notes, organize them, go up to my room, get off my phone, start working on it right away, and then reread the chapter to see if there might be something I missed, and then I...

This may seem like a petty illustration, but there are three significant features here. One, the commanding parent is being highhanded and unrelatable. Two, the parent isn't helping her child to figure out how to effectively navigate issues like this. And three, the parent is making it about her! The kid doesn't care how the mom would do it! A parent like this probably thinks she's helping by offering her personal advice, but realistically, she's being self-centered and controlling, and her kid is bound to disconnect from her (even more).

How about something like this:
Kid: Man...I don't want to work on my project.
Mom: Which class?
Kid: Biology. Ugh.
Mom: What's it about?
Kid: Proteins.
Mom: (chuckling) That sounds exciting.
Kid: It's due Friday.
Mom: How long will it take you?
Kid: Probably a few hours.
Mom: When do you want to do it?
Kid: I think I'll have time tomorrow. If I can start on it right after school, go to practice, then come back and finish, that might work. I would rather do it sooner than later.
Mom: Cool.
Kid (feeling aligned, heard, empowered, and not controlled by the authority figure): I might ask you to look it over when I'm done.

Again, the kid needs to be the one problem-solving and doing most of the talking. The more we can work on being conversational rather than presumptuously thinking our kid should be just like us and do things our way, the better. If we're lecturing or talking about ourselves, then we're being unrelatable and losing credibility.

I know most of us naturally like to talk about ourselves, but regularly referring to our own experiences doesn't hit home with tweens and teenagers. We can save those conversations for our friends, spouses, and colleagues. And, based on past experiences, if you're legitimately afraid the kid won't meet the responsibility at hand, we'll discuss the best way to address those types of problems later in the book.

The way to fix this "me, me, me" issue is to catch it when it's happening. When you repeatedly get long-winded or say "I," you're robbing your child of the opportunity to grow in maturity and responsibility. So the next time you feel inclined to interject your own opinions or personal encounters (*I this, and I think that*), stop and register: Oops. I'm starting to dominate this conversation, so how can I communicate what I'm trying to convey but be more of a functional sounding board? My child needs to speak and think. I don't need to hijack the discussion and talk about me or what I want (unless you're asked, or asked about you, or you commit to being very strategic about when to share your experiences). If you can dedicate yourself to this concept, like in the second example above, and practice it, you'll be doing your child a huge developmental service!

To summarize, when we're with our kid it's about the kid, not about us. In most situations, the less we talk, the better. I've had lots of encounters in my office where the parent is trying to be helpful or relatable by giving either a "walk five miles in the snow story" or "here's something similar that happened to me" self-centered example. The kid thinks *you never let me talk*, or in some cases, responds, "Why do you always talk about yourself? That's not helping."

Our aim is for our children to create individual solutions, feel respected, and want to listen as we tirelessly foster a home environment for our kids to prosper. The more we have back-and-forth conversations instead of commanding dialogue, the more our children become self-responsible and able to take care of business, which grows exponentially, which is great.

And remember, they know we have all the power; there's no

need for us parents to emphasize that. Being in the power seat inspires lots of individuals to start a lecture. But those of us who have been incessantly lectured by a boss know how much we hated it and shut down. Our lectures have the same effect on our kids. *The same.* This Tri-C concept is asking parents to establish the dedication to unravel an old, bad habit, and embrace a new one.

Here's the tricky part about changing behavior. What compels us to make a shift is feeling desperate when something becomes critical and nothing we're currently doing works. Can we be subpar parents and ultimately get our kids to 18-years-old? *Sure.* But you're likely reading this book because you've placed a high value on making whatever modifications needed to parent more productively. Therefore, creating real change involves our favorite concept: Commitment. A commitment to changing your mindset and consistently executing an effective approach.

When it comes to teenagers, we'd like to think that the nature of the relationship shouldn't involve so much one-sided "parental commitment" because many adolescents are mature enough to participate in how things roll with their folks. However, naturally strong-willed and ADHD kids (who are almost all hard-headed) are often delayed in their interpersonal development, and very much need their parents to almost single-handedly continue to lead the Connected Way.

The good news is the majority of these inflexible individuals warm up considerably and grow in awareness as Tri-C becomes the norm. They also tend to go through a nice developmental jump in maturity between the ages of 18- and 21-years-old, then again from 26- to 29-years-old (in my professional experience). In other words, they'll eventually get there, but it's imperative for parents to stay tolerant throughout all of child-rearing.

That said, some rigid-minded, immature adolescents I treat don't seem to know exactly what they're supposed to be doing. Or, to put it more precisely, they don't know how to convince their parents to give them what they really want: *freedom*.

I tell these teenagers they are choosing not to follow a formula that works. To give you an idea as to how many of these kids think, here's a snippet from a session (bursting with Tri-C essentials we'll work on throughout the book) with a struggling 15-year-old whose attitude had become so obnoxious that his mom told me she was ready to jump off a cliff:

Kid: My parents aren't letting me do anything.
Me: What do you mean?
Kid: My curfew is earlier than all my friends. They have to know where I am every second. I never get to do what I want. They took away Snapchat forever. (Teens love to speak in absolutes, and most everything is a big deal.)
Me: That's a bummer. It sounds like they don't trust you.
Kid: They don't.
Me: Why do you think that is?
Kid: I don't know. Because they're dumb?
Me: Ahh. Well, like how?
Kid: I don't know. Maybe because I'm failing a couple of classes right now, and they caught me vaping last week.
Me: Yeah, that would do it.
Kid: I'm sick of them.
Me: Let me ask you this. Would you say their overall expectations are fair for a 15-year-old? For parents who are trying to be responsible?
Kid: I guess...
Me: And do you know what their rules are?
Kid: I think so—but they just yell all the time.
Me: It sounds like they don't trust you because you're not meeting their expectations.

Kid: Maybe. They also nag me about doing chores.
Me: Let's figure out what's more important to you.

This discouraged 15-year-old's thinking was immature—in many ways, closer to that of an 11-year-old's. (I see this a lot with hard-headed and ADHD kids: their emotional maturity doesn't always match their age, which can clearly cause problems.) His lack of empathy was not helping.

To refresh, empathy is being able to place noticeable value on what other people want and how other people feel (in nearly any situation), and having the ability to incorporate these interpersonal skills into thinking and behavior. Remember, naturally strong-willed kids just want what they want, and if their wants don't align with what the parents require? *Problems.*

On the flip side, innately empathic kids tend to be more considerate, and although they'll have opinions and wants that differ from their folks, these kids instantly consider the entire picture of:

- My parents love me and take care of me.
- I know my parents are trying to raise me right.
- It's important to me to be respectful and honor my relationship with them.
- I need to learn how to be more self-responsible.

As mentioned earlier, children who are more heavily weighted on the "strong empathy" side of the continuum are much easier to raise, and most of their parents don't feel the need to read parenting books or show up in my office (unless something is pressing, like debilitating anxiety or depression).

However, most rigid-minded kids do not have empathic thoughts automatically whip through their heads. Over time they can learn the value of these mindful characteristics, just as smart children who are not naturally good at math can learn to understand mathematical concepts with repetition. Tri-C helps parents successfully foster their innately stubborn kids to become more mature and cooperative.

Now, back to the narrative. Instead of this 15-year-old just "giving in" to his parents, he was becoming more defiant, which made his parents angrier. If this sounds familiar, you can take the lead and help your child mentally reconfigure a successful way to take some responsibility and help fix this.

It begins with a conversation, not a lecture. Otherwise, you'll immediately get shut out. Suppose you've already launched into the Connected Way relationship. In that case, this process will be much easier because you're focused on a constructive way to communicate instead of allowing your frustration to make your head explode.

I can stay calm as the adult and talk this through. Just because my kid is acting oppositional, that is not a threat to me. I have all the power, and can address this situation effectively.

Respectfully ask *why* your teen is choosing not to meet the requirement (we'll expand on this later). State that you're not in the business of being controlling; you need to establish trust. A kid earns trust by being mature and responsible, aka, meeting the parent's reasonable expectations. The more the parent trusts the child, the more freedom is granted. *That is the "teenage" formula.*

> Me: It looks like you're more focused on doing what you want than having more freedom.
> Kid: Huh?
> (I expected that reply, especially from an inflexible thinker.)
> Me: You tell me you want as much freedom as possible.
> Kid: Yeah.
> Me: Your parents decide what you get to do, and everything goes through them, right?
> Kid: I guess.

Me: The more your parents trust you, the more they'll allow you to do what you want.

Kid: I suppose.

Me: That's the formula. If you choose to meet their conditions, your parents will be impressed and trust you more. And the more they trust you, the more overall freedom you earn. They'll see you making good choices and trust that you'll make good choices outside the home.

Kid: Part of my brain tells me to do what they say, but the other half tells me to *forget them*. They're so annoying.

Me: Yeah, I see that. It's tough to feel negative toward your folks.

Kid: What should I do?

Me: That's up to you. You tell me you want freedom, so how do you think you can do a better job of earning their trust? (Give the kid the responsibility where you can. This is a Tri-C front-line principle.)

Kid: Try harder in school?

Me: What else?

Kid: Don't vape? Do my chores?

Me: I promise your parents have better things to do than micromanage you.

Kid: My mom said the more self-discipline I have, the less they have to discipline me.

Me: You have a wise mother.

Kid: So should I do everything they say?

Me: I'm not telling you what to do, but it looks like you've got two options.

Kid: Huh?

Me: You can either start trying to meet their expectations or keep it going like it is.

Kid: Hmm...

Me: And I don't care which one you pick. I just know that when kids find the balance between doing what they want and taking

care of their responsibilities (i.e., blending their world and the real world—some kids naturally are good at this; some kids are not), parents act more positively towards them.
Kid sighs: I need to get better at that. I seem to have a hard time not getting my way. (We devoted some time in our sessions to helping him expand his perspective and see the value of being more cooperative.)
Me: Let's say you do get better at it and become a more responsible-acting teenager. How do you think that would go?
Kid: I tried that before. Nothing changed.
Me: For how long?
Kid: I don't know. Maybe a week.
Me: I know a week to you might seem like a long time, but to an adult, it's nothing. Do you want to try an experiment?
Kid: What do you mean?
Me: Today is the 12th. Let's say you try to meet their expectations the best you can until the end of the month, and see how they start treating you. And if your parents are trying...
(A literal-thinking individual does much better with concrete dialogue, dates, expressions, etc. If the kid is a black-and-white thinker, try to communicate in black-and-white terms whenever necessary. That person has trouble seeing the gray, so don't expect the kid to just "get" or accept what you're trying to say.)
Kid: I think I can do that.
Me: If you actually pull it off? Watch the magic.

The mom came back into the session, and we explained what we'd discussed. She seemed doubtful (she recognized he had some shortcomings in maturity, which I assured her would eventually develop and catch up in his 20s), but she agreed to do her part and not get emotionally provoked if he got a little snarky, and be clear and respectful (i.e., watch her delivery) throughout this exercise. I explained that they both wanted the same thing: for him to earn freedom through her trust.

Because the mom dedicated herself to creating a new communication template her kid could more easily follow, eventually, the relationship began to switch from "me vs. you" to a feeling of "we're in the same corner." Not only did the adolescent begin to see the value of meeting his parents' expectations (it took more than a few weeks to come to fruition, but we certainly got the ball rolling), this kid also realized how great it was when his parent(s) felt favorable towards him, and vice versa.

The key is:

It started with Mom. She trained herself to recognize she couldn't come at him any longer in a Directive "do what I say" way. Instead, she focused on modifying her delivery and implemented an overall change in her fundamental communication style.

After another week had passed, they came back to the office.

"You guys are smiling," I said. "That's nice to see."

Fear: Most parents sincerely desire to be great caregivers. A serious factor that compromises good parenting (not caused by a muleheaded child who makes us want to pull out our hair) is the powerful beast known as fear. Fear often shows up as control, meaning fear-based parenting tendencies manifest in one of two ways:

1. Helicopter or lawnmower parents who restrict growth by inappropriately enabling or protecting the kid from ordinary life challenges.

2. Insecure, over-involved parents whose distorted senses of worth are somehow tied to the child's achievement, and/or they vicariously live through their child. They fear if the kid doesn't do almost everything their way,

then success will not be achieved, control will be lost, and the young human will shame the parent or family.

These ill-advised approaches cripple most of what we're trying to accomplish: to raise a confident individual. We know it's critical for a child to experience natural failures as the result of poor decision making or lack of effort (which some of us parents can have a hard time allowing), as areas of essential development are fostered from misfires. When we over-control, we are interacting disrespectfully. We inhibit the young person's development and defy an important parental objective: to help advance self-confidence. The child is not allowed sufficient ownership to figure out enough things independently.

"Mama! Waaah! I fell and scraped my knee!"

"Oh my gosh! My poor baby! I think I see a little blood. We better go to the doctor and get you some antibiotics!"

Stop! We don't overreact and give our children antibiotics for knee scrapes. We allow their bodies to do what they're designed to do: heal on their own and learn to fight off infections. *Same concept.*

Many parents in my office have admitted their anxiety consistently gets the best of them, and they know they control or coddle too much, but they don't know what to do about it. Have no fear! (*Ha!*)

Tri-C helps offset excessive policing, enabling, and disappointment by teaching the parent to interact the right way. The more we respond the right way, the more motivated the child is to be responsible. And the more responsible our kid acts, the more comfortable we are to grant independence. As you dedicate yourself to looking at your kid through a clear lens, you will know better when to step in or when to leave it be.

This book is heavy in addressing the counterproductive aspects of scolding and over-controlling and how those approaches negatively impact children. I also assume you want to avoid raising incompetent kids or entitled brats. Try to only do for your kids what they cannot do for themselves. There is a difference between being nice and being enabling.

For example, I am not promoting healthy development by carrying my child's backpack, allowing my teenager's room to always look like a bomb went off, buying that kid nearly everything that's desired or not providing/requiring opportunities to make money, fixing every meal, doing my child's homework, allowing profanity at home, doing my adolescent's laundry, ordering at restaurants for my tween, issuing minimal to zero chores, being the kid's personal assistant, or fighting every battle. So remember to try and stay respectful with your words and your overall "empowering not enabling" parental style. When we enable, we make it about the parent rather than the child's advancement. Most of you already know how harmful this enabling stuff can be, but sometimes it's good to hear it from someone else.

Here's something I occasionally see in my office. For some adults, a big part of their identity is wrapped up in being "a parent," which compels them to chronically over-parent from day one. Not good. And for other adults, as their parenting duties gradually diminish each year, it feels like a threat—a threat to their significance. Therefore, many of these people experience an identity crisis and will exercise their parental importance inappropriately by over-controlling or coddling when their kids do not need their influence.

We can train ourselves to not be dictators and/or to not enable. As stated previously, there are numerous aspects of good parenting that do not come naturally (at first), but through dedication to executing these fundamental concepts, *success will follow.*

I always tell kids in my office that their number one priority is to take care of themselves; but as parents, **our number one priority is to take care of our children**. However, to do it and do it well, we must also do a nice job tending to ourselves. We had a life before kids, we still need a life while being parents, and we'll have a life after our children are grown. We cannot act like a parental martyr or an enabling champion—we would be making it about us. And people see through those fabrications anyway.

Parenting is an endless challenge, and a worn-out version of you is not good. Set up date nights. Find good babysitters. Send your kids to camps or reputable community centers/programs. Let them sleep over at solid relatives' and friends' houses. Establish some comfort in thinking "everything is going to be okay" as you create breaks to help refuel your mind and body. Do not take this lightly: You also deserve to enjoy life.

The better you are individually, the better of a human you will be with your kids. When we're personally not doing good, it's incredibly difficult to parent appropriately. There's an old saying in the mental health industry that has significant truth to it: *Children are only as healthy as their parents.*

Clear

Before we discuss looking at your child objectively and communicating clear, reasonable expectations, I want to mention this:

You and your kid are different from other parent-child pairings, and I cannot instruct you on every possible situation that's going to arise. Let's switch the analogy from playing guitar back to golf. Child-rearing is like being a professional golfer (i.e., you are a professional parent), and I'm your golf coach.

I can rigorously work with you on the driving range, play practice rounds, and give you as many lessons as you want/need (i.e., you can read this book as deeply and as many times as you want/need). But I can't accompany you every time you play in tournaments and direct you on how to approach every shot best. Nor will I pompously express my opinions (on the golf course or in this manual) regarding subject matter such as politics, religion, dating, abortion, or sexuality/gender-based concerns. Your child will ultimately look to you regarding what is appropriate and what is not regarding various topics.

Tri-C is not a far-reaching, parenting master plan to overwhelm or "fix" you, nor is it an amateur, Whac-A-Mole approach from a pseudo-professional or clever mom or dad who amusingly tries to convince you how to raise your kids. Tri-C is a formal system, a methodology of parenting specifically designed to soak into your core and provide you with in-depth, foundational changes where necessary.

Of course, you'll experience a learning curve and that's totally normal. As long as your child knows you are committed and you eventually master the economical yet powerful Tri-C fundamentals, your parenting confidence will grow. Tri-C helps you tip the scales, so eventually the vast majority of communication with your kid is not administrative, contentious, or bossy, and you and your child get to fully enjoy each other's company. I mean, isn't that the entire point of having a kid in the first place?

However, after reading this book, if you think for some reason there are certain areas of parenting you're still unsure about, you can find specific videos, articles, podcasts, etc., by *qualified* medical and mental health professionals who should be able to help. Do some research and make sure they're legitimate players in the industry. I also recognize that some of you might struggle with family or community support. Understand that Tri-C is merely constructed to show you best how to parent individually, as I've tried to create an approach that compensates for as many external obstacles as possible.

A Quick Fundamentals Review

I was talking (again) with a very Compassionate Boss mom in my office. She was painfully stuck in the frustrated headspace of: My kid just needs to do what I say! Things were disintegrating. But then, as we talked back-and-forth and I continued to convey the Tri-C philosophy, it "clicked." I witnessed a transformation. It was awesome. She finally came to understand there's a specific, effective culture of parenting.

She reflected, "You know, I had to *learn* how to productively interact with all the clients I see."

"And you're very successful," I replied.

"You're essentially saying the same thing. There's a correct way to do it."

Let's take a look at what we've discussed so far, and notice, some of these principles you'll see again in some fashion:

- You have more influence than anything or anybody.
- Kids and the art of parenting are not as confusing as they're made out to be.
- Tri-C consistency is paramount and will ultimately foster success.
- Some children are naturally agreeable, some are not.
- Stay calm and respectful, and your kid will perpetually follow your lead.
- **Do not get worked up because you don't have to; you have all the power.**
- Raising another human being is the most important endeavor you will ever experience.
- Fiercely honor your relationship no matter what is happening. Never act ugly or say mean things to your child. Never. The world will unfortunately do plenty of that.
- Life now is about what your kid needs more than what you want.
- Train yourself to create conversations instead of lectures.
- Enabling or taking yourself too seriously (or not effectively addressing *your* issues) is selfish and impedes your child's development.

Meeting Expectations

This entire concept is big, and this chapter is long, so here we go. If the kid is choosing to meet a responsibility, then fortunately, the parent does not need to intervene. For example, if your child independently wakes up, has breakfast, executes hygiene, gathers everything needed for the school day, gets ready on time, etc., no parenting is required. Your kid realizes there is value in performing the morning duties. You do not have to promote your anxiety or arrogance and needlessly chime in and remind your child about anything (unless there's something unique happening that day), as that would generate negative feelings towards you. Your goal is to raise a self-responsible person who listens to you regarding relevant matters and wants to have a great relationship.

News flash! Children are not as mature as adults and do not always choose to meet reasonable expectations because they're just goofy kids. Often what they want and what parents want aren't the same thing. In other words, there will be some natural, built-in contention. That's fine—we wouldn't expect otherwise—we have to get okay with it and deal with it appropriately. Happily, for some parents, their responsible children seem to value meeting the majority of normal requirements. There may be occasional pushback and mischievousness, but not a lot. These kids understand it's in their best interest to do what's asked.

Other kids, not so much.

What happens when people don't effectively learn how to meet responsibilities? The real world beats them down. You do not want any of your children to take that kind of beating. Therefore, it is your assignment to help your kid(s) "connect the dots" and understand more clearly what's being communicated and see the merit in doing what's required.

But first (here it comes again), it's incredibly important to accurately identify what type of human you've got on your hands. I have engaged in countless conversations in my office with frustrated parents about this, and the Q & A segment of my seminars often evolve into back-and-forth discussions, encouraging parents to hone their ability to look at their kid clearly and stop fantasizing about who they want their child to be.

Expecting a non-athletic kid to be a starter on the football team, a hard-headed child to have big-picture thinking, or a non-brainiac kid to make the National Honor Society isn't realistic. Tri-C dictates that if you can perceive your child objectively, your expectations of life skills, level of maturity, and willingness to comply will become accurate. As the parent, you'll dedicate your efforts to shaping your child's natural strengths (build, build, build), not wish for a different or "better subject" to mold.

What I'm about to state is a very important parenting fundamental: Regardless of how your child is wired, you can create and staunchly maintain normal, reasonable expectations, and get that person to learn how to become solid and responsible. (Unless the child, or in some cases the parent, truly does have a "considerable issue.") And, of course, your expectations will be age-appropriate and expand as the child grows older. It's the lack of maturity and willingness to meet expectations that gets parents confused. Your kid being receptive and meeting your requirements are mostly based on three things you control: 1) the specific words and delivery used in how you communicate, 2) your consistency, and 3) the nature of the relationship. Welcome to Tri-C world.

Here's a basic example when a kid noticeably is choosing to not do what's asked:

> Parent: Turn off that video game and come set the table.
> Child doesn't respond.
> Parent: Hey, let's go. Come on.
> Child: In a minute...
> Parent: I said right now.
> Child remains glued to the screen.
> Parent: Turn off that stupid game! Why don't you mind me!
> Child: Okay! I'm coming! Sheesh!
> (Now upset, the parent feels disrespected and takes it personally after years of occasional and normal childhood non-compliance.)
> Parent: I don't understand why you won't do what I say! I cook you dinner and you don't even care!

This parent is failing to consider the audience. Dr. Gary Landreth, a king of child-centered play therapy (a very effective style of therapy for younger children when executed correctly), states that parents must be careful not to view their kids as "miniature adults," as expectations will rarely be met when that happens. Frustration strikes when unrealistic expectations are not met, compelling parents to "strike out" at their children. It can be very destructive.

And for lots of "normal" parents with "normal" kids, the problem is the adults feeling as though they have to force maturity instead of letting it grow organically, which in time, it will.

"I need to teach my boys to become men. They need to get up at the crack of dawn and mow the yard! What's wrong with them!"

To which I smile and respond, "They're not men yet; they're barely teenagers. How many kids do we know who are jumping to cut the grass?" *They'll ultimately cut the grass because they know they have to. You can be cool about it.*

Again, when we choose to become parents, it is no longer about us. ("You hurt my feelings!" Or, "You made me mad!") It's about: What does my child need from me right now so I can effectively accomplish the two primary parental tasks: to protect and to develop? (Here's a hint: Your kid will be much more inclined to receive your 18 years of cultivation if you work to consistently be respectful instead of being rude).

Although the "set the table" scenario above doesn't involve protection, how could the parent better accept the kid's normal level of maturity and communicate more effectively to foster positive development?:

Parent: Would you please turn off your game and come set the table?
Child doesn't respond.

Parent: Hey, let's go.
Child: In a minute.
Parent: Now, please.
Child is transfixed.
Parent: Come on, it's ready.
Child remains unresponsive.
Parent: Come set the table, or you'll choose not to play video games tomorrow.
Child gets up and sets the table.

In this example, the parent administered a basic approach that somewhat reflects the classic *Parenting with Love and Logic* technique. It works smoothly with naturally agreeable kids because they understand the expectation is fair, and the parent proposed a reasonable arrangement. The reason it works smoothly with self-willed kids (if you feel this strategy wouldn't be effective, hold tight, we'll get you there) is because of the black-and-whiteness of the requirement with no room for loopholes or confusion. The parent clearly understood that the recipient was just a kid who did not have the maturity of an adult, and the parent cared about communicating respectfully so the child would be receptive to meeting the expectation. (Regarding something bigger like mowing the yard, let the kid pick what day/time to do it if there's not some kind of time crunch. As long as it's done regularly and done well, that's what really matters. It's called "partnering," which we'll speak to later in this chapter.)

The bottom line: It worked (or will work). The child performed the task, and the parent maintained credibility. The sensible, skilled parent honored a practical strategy instead of honoring the common, inappropriate default of wishing the kid were a certain way. To allow your child to hurt your feelings or wish that a young human could magically be more mature is a huge no-no.

Aside from having a delightful relationship where kids want to oblige the respectful-acting parent, what's the biggest reason this simple application consistently does the job? *Children know when the parent means business.* For lots of youngsters to understand that the parent means business, a consequence has to be executed at a very early point in this paradigm. And there's a specific, Tri-C way to properly dish out the medicine that we'll get to in a bit.

Humans respond most effectively to consequences, and whether we like it or not, that's just the way we are. I hear lots of parents groan about their kids not doing what they're told after they've been asked a few times, instead of recognizing the fact that people (children) would rather do what they want, not necessarily what others (parents) want them to do.

"I shouldn't have to take her phone to make her clean her room. I've been asking for three days, and it's still a mess!" (How many kids want to clean their room, load the dishes, or do yard work?)

But, when parents teach themselves not to get flustered and administer a consequence or verbalize the legitimate threat of one to encourage their kids to meet certain responsibilities (or "to partner," again, coming soon), compliance ensues. What a concept, right?

Here's a glimpse of "partnering" but the parent undermines it:

Dad: Take your shoes to your room.
Daughter: Can I grab them when I go upstairs? I'm going to bed in just a little while.
Dad: I guess.
(A few minutes pass.)
Dad: I'm sick of looking at your shoes!
Daughter: I thought you said I could take them when I go to bed?
Dad: I'm tired of you leaving your stuff all over the house!
Daughter: But you said—

Dad: I'm done with this conversation. Pick them up!

This type of communication approach is unfortunately common, especially when a parent is tired or feeling negative or annoyed for some reason. The dad is completely disregarding the relationship and totally satisfying his own wants! That's disrespect and arrogance at its finest.

The Tri-C goal is for us parents to get over ourselves, stop our sour emotions from escalating, and quickly recognize what's more important: A) Honoring the relationship with my kid (who was going to perform the request), or B) *Getting my way right now!* My guess is all normal parents would answer, "Honoring the relationship." This is very fixable; it just takes a commitment to our kid's well-being. (And if she did forget to take her shoes, there's an appropriate way to address that, which we'll cover.)

Nearly all children know the differences between good/bad, right/wrong, fair/unfair, and reasonable/ unreasonable—do not think otherwise. But even if your kids understand your requirements are normal and cannot justifiably argue with them, they might not *like* them, and you might have to build in some consequences (or strong reminders) along the way.

That's a good thing. Life at home is much better when parents get into what works rather than getting upset because they have dreams of their kids being flush with adult maturity. I'm not sure which planet where that's the deal, but it sure ain't this one.

Regarding a short-sighted child who can regularly tend to wrestle with cooperating, the parent must learn that always going hard in a traditional "I say jump, you say how high" approach **does not work**. Because the adult clearly has all the power, it simply boils down to the parent downloading the Tri-C mental recalibration: Change the lens to perceive the child objectively, minimize frustration, and learn to exercise authority constructively. The kid cannot justifiably get mad if the parent merely is acting responsibly and executing a fair consequence or calmly reinforcing a reminder—and the young human knows it. Let me say that again: *The child knows it.*

More simply, don't allow yourself to get upset if your kid isn't instantly doing whatever it is you're asking, because when you get upset, you potentially damage the relationship, lose credibility, and deteriorate respect. Realize what type of kid you've got—either more clueless or cooperative—and start with a brief chat to determine if there's simply a communication breakdown (which, in all honesty, is relatively common).

But if rules or expectations consistently are not being followed, then give that child a choice to either take care of it or experience an appropriate penalty. The Tri-C method moves the focus from your kid not complying, to focusing on how to keep your cool and handle the situation effectively—incentivizing your child to meet expectations as you keep your likability front and center. The more likable you are, the more your kiddo will progressively and automatically want to do what you say.

One more time: If you initiate a respectful discussion utilizing your adult conversation skills, you might illuminate that the issue can be worked out peacefully!

You: Do you want to mow on Saturday or Sunday?
Son: I guess Saturday.
You: Okay, but we're going to your grandparents at two, which means you'll need to start by twelve o'clock. Good?
Son: That's cool.

If your kid naturally is more responsible/mature, then you'll most likely hear the lawnmower fire up in the morning. But you know your child, and if that kid is somewhat immature or forgetful, you might need to issue a respectful reminder if there's no movement from him as the clock quickly approaches noon. *And that's totally fine.*

But if you uncover that your kid is clearly choosing to be defiant, you can execute a fair consequence or the threat of one (which must have follow-through). Be mindful of your delivery. How we deliver is just as impactful as the punishment—we must be careful and not be ugly about it. A constructive delivery means we essentially learn to be non-emotional every time our kid is acting out or slow to comply, and we're forced to issue a ruling or a reminder. This is where we become transactional instead of emotional.

But sometimes I'll hear parents say, "I'm an emotional person. It's hard for me to not get upset when my child is being argumentative, uncooperative, or disrespectful." I get that. But as alluded to earlier, learning the Tri-C approach takes a little work. Thankfully the blueprint is here, just keep turning these pages. A great thing to keep in mind is that Tri-C is designed to help the child become much more agreeable and respectful *over time*, which minimizes parental opportunities to get angry in the first place!

How about an example:

> Mom, who can see that her 9th grade daughter isn't in the best mood as they're driving home from school: How many questions were on your math quiz?
> Kid responds with a little attitude: Like I'm supposed to remember that?
>
> **Stop!** The mom has two choices. She can either allow herself to get upset with her child for being snarky and respond negatively...
> Mom: Don't talk to me like that! I just asked you a question!
> **(WRONG)**

The parent instantly threw gas on the fire as she made it about her.

Or she can quickly switch on the adult maturity component in her brain and respond appropriately:

Mom, who can see that her 9th grade daughter isn't in the best mood as they're driving home from school: How many questions were on your math quiz?
Kid responds with a little attitude: Like I'm supposed to remember that?
Mom: *Hey.*
Kid: I'm sorry. I'm just having a bad day.
(CORRECT)
The mom did not allow her 14-year-old to hurt her feelings, but instead focused on her kid's development and maintaining a good relationship. Do not be remiss: the daughter also quickly recognized her mom chose to be cool instead of ugly, which gives the parent more credibility, which inspires the child to become more respectful in all situations as she grows in maturity and mindfulness. Wins everywhere.

As I suggested earlier, certain kids might be struggling with something that's impeding their ability to act more pleasant, like anxiety, ADHD, some inconspicuous, yet influential measure of mild autism, or depression (people who are depressed can regularly experience periods of anger or "I don't care," which is real). These diagnoses can restrict our ability to function well or be willing to accommodate. If your child is becoming more surly or disconnected over the course of a few months, but you're doing a nice job executing Tri-C, some underlying anxiety and/or depression might be emerging. Time to get that checked. Seriously.

To add, in my professional opinion, about 25% of our population demonstrate various degrees of autism spectrum-like traits (e.g., rigid thinking, inability to adjust easily, some awkwardness, takes things too literally, and somewhat short on empathy and social awareness). I'm not declaring that an entire quarter of the human race could formally be diagnosed as autistic, but lots of individuals exhibit these characteristics. Also, be advised that many spectrum features usually minimize with age and experience.

Regarding ADHD, a major amount of these kids exhibit noticeable immaturity, natural impulsiveness, forgetfulness, disorganization, and stubbornness—all characteristics that hinder awareness and push parents to madness. Parents of an ADHD child must exercise great patience and never dismiss the reality that this mental/learning difference creates challenges.

Here's an email that a mom sent to me before she brought in her son. She wanted me to know some of the behaviors that were happening. For a number of you, this is going to sound familiar:

Main Issues:
-Suspected ADHD/autistic traits
- Problems with listening and following simple instructions
- Needs constant reminders for everyday tasks
- Uncontrollable emotions
- Constant complaining and excuses in all situations (even during fun activities)
- Doesn't always recognize social cues and will occasionally act out or say inappropriate things
- Lying
- Disrespectfulness—always arguing and believing he is right
- Laziness—knowing he has responsibilities but doesn't want to do them

The short-tempered frustration towards a kid like this creates more issues, which we're trying to eliminate. In other words, incorrect interactions towards a kid like this make everything worse! Parents of an ADHD or "spectrumy" child must loyally stay in the business of being understanding and not give in to their own anger and disappointment. If they chronically succumb to their inaccurate expectations and don't learn how to interact the correct (Tri-C) way, the relationship ends up in the sewer. *So long, successful parenting.*

Also, a kid might have more than one formal diagnosis (comorbidity) to discern that requires a strong parent-child connection, and a possible need for professional help. This is another reason why it's critical that you perceive your young human accurately. The better your relationship, the more you'll have clear back-and-forth conversations, and the more astutely you'll grasp your child.

Let's move forward and talk about parenting predicaments that might be a little more difficult. When our kids choose to act ill-mannered, it is our Tri-C task to stay calm, create respectful dialogue, and oftentimes ask "why." Asking why can be an important piece of tactical parenting. Regardless of how far they're pegged on the stubborn/immature scale, even kids who are mildly tempered can become obstinate over time if they've been "allowed" to. Remember, many children will try to get away with numerous things until they realize they can't. I know it's annoying behavior, but it's super normal.

When contention between you and your child is starting to brew, you can turn your emotional dial to "off," stay unfazed, and open a potential powder keg interaction using a conversational, concerned question like, "Hey man, what's up?" This approach means you've created a specific, non-defensive delivery of two things:

1. I'm being super cool about this, and you are not (and nobody likes to be the you-know-what).

2. We are not going to argue, and I'm actually curious—not shaming, sarcastic, or condescending—as to why you're choosing to act this way. And, because I'm the parent, I can frame this interaction however I want (i.e., Connected Way) and ultimately understand and/or win whatever is going on between us. *Ahh, the comfort of having (appropriate) control.*

The stage has been set for a chat, not a fight. (Know this: If your kid is rigid-minded to any degree, that person most likely cannot process your sarcasm; it is too gray and potentially insulting, and we don't do anything to wound our children. I've had parents in my office actually boast about their sarcastic humor, so please understand that lots of kids can probably dish it out but can't take it. Consider training yourself to eliminate it entirely from your family dialogue and save it for your friends. With our children, it's too easily misconstrued and hurtful.)

If your earnest questioning/conversation works and the intractable child has a flash of maturity and abides, that's a nice win-win. But sometimes the kid doesn't have enough internal motivation to meet the expectation and **talk is cheap** (typical with a hardheaded child). The little whippersnapper might need an actual consequence to reach an important understanding.

If that's the case, you will not bat an eye and create enough external incentive (a consequence or the legitimate threat of one) for your kid to realize doing what's asked is a much better option. Recognize that words and emotions tend to be abstract and can conveniently be misinterpreted by the child; therefore, this approach is very black and white—just like how a headstrong individual tends to see the world.

Know that rewards are also great motivators—as long as they're used fittingly. Tap into your natural instincts on when to offer a reward to inspire your child to meet a requirement. Do not be reluctant to do this because, with consequences and rewards, we're just shaping behavior. When our frustration drives us to deliver unceasing consequences, it's like beating a junkyard dog—the creature only becomes more resentful. Consider offering some type of bounty for a responsibility being met. When the child meets the standard (e.g., "If you do your homework all week without me having to force you, we'll go to laser tag this weekend."), that's another win-win. After you implement this bonus strategy a number of times or weeks in a row, the expected behavior usually becomes routine, making the reward no longer necessary because the kid "gets it." Rewards are very effective when incorporated properly.

But be aware that if you set the appropriate bonus too far in the future, some children can't see it and it will lose its draw. Toward the end of the day or week is good for most younger kids. You can push the prize out a bit further for tweens and teens.

However, if a reward is not suitable or won't do the trick, you can issue a fair consequence that is more powerful to your child than upholding the defiance. Many parents implement a reward-consequence combo if the situation calls for it, meaning the child's choice of behavior will bring either a gift or a punishment—just like in the real world.

Let's have a little fun and expand on this Tri-C procedure. Here's a consequence-only example. "Your" immature, uninspired tween son agrees to shower every night. It's not happening. You justifiably feel irritated. You can:

A) Quarrel, yell, and punish, which is highly undesirable and drives the kid to become even more insufferable. (*Down, down, down you go...you know the rest.*)

B) As you begin the new Tri-C learning process for your kid, sincerely (not angrily) ask why your child is choosing not to recognize this normal requirement.

In all reality, regarding an example like this, a 10- to 12-year-old should be mature enough to know the value of showering every day, and it shouldn't be an issue. But for some, that's not the case. If you've been in similar situations (i.e., your child not meeting other simple rules/chores/hygiene), you've probably done everything you thought you could to convince your kid to stop being oppositional and fulfill the normal expectation. Moving forward and implementing the full-force Tri-C process might feel a little alien at first; however, *you are primed and ready.*

Here we go: If you choose B, then hopefully your stubborn kid will have a self-aware, mature realization of "I don't want to do this, but I know I need to," and the task is performed. However, in the first few enactments of Tri-C, you might hear a weak excuse or some ill-mannered answer like, "Because it's stupid!" Or, "I'm too tired!" Or an actual fib, "I already did."

If that's the case, do not argue. Because if you do:

Gas! Fire! Boom! Bad!

Your naturally challenging child knows this requirement is fair but is trying to get away with not doing it for whatever reason. But by initiating your new mental recalibration (this is just a game you're playing—try not to get wound up or take any of this seriously as you squirt water on the fire, not spray it with gasoline), you keep this interaction conversational and stay in the reasonable part of your brain. If you lose your patience and get forceful, you immediately enter the onramp to the freeway of failure.

A quirky child can have quirky thinking. Maybe the kid only likes to shower in the morning; he doesn't like to shower because of sensory issues and the shampoo or soap feels "weird"; he doesn't like the towel texture; he hates to feel cold while drying off—it could be a million things. Talk it over and stay cool because you know your kid is a little peculiar. Help him figure out a way to best meet the requirement. (Or negotiate—maybe taking a shower in the morning is okay with you.) Keep your mind calm, see what the deal is, and don't allow the issue to become an argument.

When you stay level-headed and patient (as much as you possibly can), your kid will eventually follow your lead, drop the defensiveness, think reasonably, and figure out a way to navigate these kinds of "shower things" with a helpful conversation. Almost all problems can be worked out with a discussion when the parent chooses to be a mature adult and to not feel *my authority is being threatened*! if the kid isn't automatically compliant.

However, sometimes this approach takes a little while to sink in, and things at home don't go so smoothly. Peaceful conversations don't quite work until Tri-C is the family theme. In that case, a child who is still choosing to be defiant and dig in, realizing the new Tri-C parent is not going to be drawn into a debate, will feel distressed as the juicy opportunity to get that adult upset or to have any control is vanishing. I once had a little maverick in my office smile as he admitted that if he can get his mom to argue, she's stepped into "his territory."

If refusal is the *stance du jour*, after your kid's laughable answer to the original question of why he won't shower—simply ask the question again. If it becomes clear your child will not engage in a productive discussion and does not want to comply, then you'll coolly say, "You can choose to do it, or you'll lose your screens tomorrow."

You both know this is not an end-of-the-world punishment your child might choose to suffer, but now it's officially become a contest. Your kid may become angrier, attempt to defend the chosen position, and say more dumb things like, "Why do you care?!"

To that, you will calmly counter, "We've already discussed this, but if you need me to tell you once more, I will." (Your child always has the right to ask why. Regardless of whether there's "an attitude" or not, try never to respond with, "Because I said so." That is discounting and it damages the relationship that you are trying to build. You're always upholding the relationship because you love your child unconditionally and because you know that a maintained, positive connection makes parenting 5,000 times easier.)

Your exasperated youngster may continue to argue; however, you will keep this encounter in perspective, not take the kid seriously, and **not respond at all because you don't have to. The consequence will do the talking for you. If you keep responding, you're providing ammunition for both you and your kid to get more upset. Down you go.**

(Did you notice where I mentioned, "Not take the kid seriously?")

—Your child will gawk at you in anticipation of your retort.

—You will maintain an expressionless face as you try not to laugh at this toothless wonder trying to act tough.

—Your kid will react to your non-provoked stance with another dopey, disrespectful comeback.

Then, as you casually return to what you were doing and not allow this to break into a death spiral, you'll say, "We don't talk like that to each other in this family. Try again. And let me know what you decide."

If your kid continues to be contentious, you can ignore it or respond with a very brief, canned answer. This can be difficult until you learn what to say, but the lesson is coming soon. Your child will make a brutish attempt to goad you, and every fiber of you might be tempted to jump into the ring, go toe-to-toe, and cut that joker down to size. If you do ignite, argue, or lock yourself in your room, then you lose, child wins.

If you stay calm and quiet, you will experience victory! You'll get to witness the beauty of your powerless kiddo tasting bitter defeat as the tween eventually skulks off and is left with a wrenching decision to either shower or lose privileges. This is a glorious and potentially defining moment. And, if this is one of your early encounters with this type of parenting strategy, your kid might not perform the requirement at hand due to inherent immaturity, an unwillingness to lose, or hopes that you won't actually administer the consequence.

Let's say he doesn't shower. So what? The kid is getting ready for bed while you've stayed super collected. You also know that when tomorrow comes, all screen privileges have disappeared, and *that's when real change begins to take shape*. Because you will enact the consequence, your child will either accept it or get upset.

Again, so what? Unless the kid is going to do something dangerous like jump out the window, you can either sit there and watch the circus act, or go do something else.

You're creating a new precedent for all situations like this. And what helps keep you from overreacting and flipping your ignition switch throughout this entire interaction is that you are committed to the Tri-C process, which means A) you know your kid will have future opportunities to possibly demonstrate bullheadedness and experience "effective learning," and B) you will stay in control of your emotions and administer this same, fruitful application when a rule is broken or an expectation is not met. By executing this approach every time, you are carving a new compliance path the child can actually traverse. Because here's what that little pistol eventually starts to realize:

Consequences stink!
It's not worth it!

You have all the power, and the more you uphold this protocol, the easier overall parenting eventually becomes. Recognize that enacting any substantial process takes time to play out, and remember to be patient as the Tri-C principles work their influence over a few weeks. (If you're dealing with a teenager, it might take a few months.) Because you exhibited such composure throughout the entire exchange, your child justifiably can't be mad at you and wrongly shift some of the blame. He knows he's supposed to shower, but you are helping him change the culture in his mind of how to perceive you. You are no longer a "threat." You are simply being a responsible parent.

Crud! My parent was cool about it (huff, huff, huff)! But now that I'm thinking...hmm, it's nice to get along with my folks, be okay meeting responsibilities, feel good about myself...

Take this approach every time because consistency is the name of the game—I can't emphasize this enough. When defiance appears, your Tri-C application and the steady stream of potentially losing privileges or delivered consequences will become so utterly convincing that it will override your child's need to be defiant. But if your kid tries to oppose you and you go back to your old ways of *I'm the parent, do what I say!* you will come across as the "bad guy," provide ammo for your kid to place blame on you, foster a child vs. parent dynamic (which is bad), and disrupt the entire regimen. Down you go.

You'll know it's working when your child no longer demonstrates bold resistance or gets upset when you uphold a normal expectation. Your kid will either meet the requirement without being asked, or mirror your response, "I know. If I don't take a shower (or whatever the task happens to be), I choose to blah, blah, blah. I get it." Smiles all around.

I've seen many discouraged parents in my office tell me they've tried a "soft" approach and proclaim it isn't effective. I actually have to lure them back to feeling hopeful and assure them since they are learning a new parenting method, they can start to experience success.

Sometimes in initial parent sessions, I'll hear, "We've already done all that, and it doesn't work."

What I'd like to say back to them is, "Yes it does. You're just not doing it right." But of course I don't say that. What I will do is teach them to drop the antiquated, *I'm the parent; mind me!* theme, then execute the Tri-C system exactly. Understand this, especially when you first begin Tri-C: If you can embrace this philosophy, be consistent, relentlessly uphold your new mindset, and employ this productive process just as it's described in this book, your kid will come around because that child will have no choice but to do so, thanks to your respectful, uniform approach.

"But Brian, I shouldn't have to be the one to change and do all this. I'm busy and worn out! Why can't my children just do what they're told!"

I know, sometimes constructive parenting can be tough (at first), but stay with it. Why? Because this works.

Delivery: I know we've already talked a little about delivery, but we'll discuss it a bit more because it's such a big deal. Storytime: I saw a nice couple a few months ago for a parent-only session regarding their son. After we sat down, the mom said, "He is such a smart, funny, and creative kid! He does well in school. We are just struggling at home trying to raise him to be a respectful and dependable young man."

Although they were desperate, I could tell they were not happy that they needed professional help—I understand that, but it almost felt as though the dad wanted to prove they had the most impossible kid of all time. After a few minutes, I realized their child wasn't super defiant, just naturally willful, and I told them I'd treated multitudes of families just like theirs.

As the conversation went back and forth, they gave examples of various issues they were having, and I would explain how to handle them. Each time, Dad would cut me off and robotically declare, "We've done that. We've tried that. Nothing works." I think this father was attempting to prove that coming to see me was a waste of time, they were competent parents, and their 13-year-old was an anomaly. The dad's frustration and his old school mindset were initially overriding his ability to look at his youngster through a clear lens and consider Tri-C.

In all honesty, some of their parenting methods were solid, but where they were dropping the ball was in their lack of consistency, follow through, and the ever-crucial delivery. How we communicate as authority figures is especially important when the spite wedge (which you'll learn about in the following section) between parents and kid has developed.

I continued to cover some fundamentals with this couple as it finally began to sink in:

> Me: Give me another issue you're having. You said it's tough getting him to do his chores?
> Mom: Yes. He won't do them.
> Me: What do you mean? He'll tell you, "No?"
> Mom: Not exactly. We'll ask him to do something, and he "forgets" or gives us some grief.
> Dad: If I'd done that when I was a kid? That would've been bad for me. My dad would've—
> Mom: We talked about this and we don't spank our kids.
> Dad: Well, maybe if we did...
> Mom: Just because you were parented that way doesn't mean we have to.
> Me: Hold on. I'm glad you don't spank. That makes our kids not like us, and the most powerful ingredient that motivates kids to want to mind is when they like us. What's a specific chore he struggles with?
> Mom: I enjoy walking the dogs, so we don't make him do that, but he's supposed to scoop dog poop every couple of days. Our dogs are big, and the backyard is small, and if it's not picked up regularly, then it gets tracked in.

Me: How long does it take him?
Dad: One minute. Maybe two. The scooper and trash can are right there.
Me: How does the conversation typically go?
Dad: I tell him to scoop the poop!
Me: What does he say?
Dad: He says he's busy or huffs and puffs or asks if he can do it later. He always has some excuse. And I'll tell you again, Doc, we've already tried to punish him for not doing it: taken his phone, computer, video games. He says he doesn't care.
Me: I think he cares. He just wants you to *think* he doesn't.
Mom: You're probably right.
Me: How about this? In his mind, it seems like it has become a "kid-versus-parents" ordeal. Let's make your exchanges feel more conversational. A big piece of this parenting approach has to do with delivery, as in, "I can be pleasant and communicate with you in a specific manner, so you'll be receptive to me." I always tell parents that almost everything can be articulated in a relaxed style.
Mom: Like walking on eggshells?
Me: Absolutely not. Talk with him in a *respectful way*. Because he has a hard time with empathy and seeing the big picture, he probably gets defensive easily.
Mom: You can say that again!
Me: Kids wired like him can tend to feel like they're being attacked, and if truth be told, it's also "convenient" to feel that way. He knows you have all the power, but in his immature thinking, he's just trying to defend himself and get what he wants.
Dad: So what do you mean exactly? Talk to him like how?
Me: Sit down with him later tonight, be very casual, and say something like, "Hey, I know this scoop poop thing has become an issue. Would you rather do it in the mornings or

when you get home from school?"
Mom: Ahh, so ask him.
Me: Yes. With an affable tone of voice. Your delivery is huge. He already knows he has to do it, but now you're being cool, and, allowing him to have some say in the matter. If the conversation is couched like nothing more than a friendly chat, it doesn't give him a clear path to become defensive.
Mom: And it helps him feel like he's got some say in the matter.
Me: Sure! You're just changing the "set up"—not your expectations. How would he answer?
Dad: He'd say he'll do it in the mornings.
Me: So tomorrow morning before leaving for school, casually ask him if he's scooped. He'll say, "Not yet." Then you'll say, "Okay, we got about 10 minutes." Then go back to what you were doing.
Dad: He won't do it.
Me: Just a second—we're not done. About three to five minutes before leaving, you'll stand by the backdoor, call for him, and ask him very nicely, "Can you come here for a second?" He shows up, you open the backdoor, smile and say, "The dog poop is waiting." He might declare, "I don't have time!" but you'll stand there with your hand on the doorknob.
Mom grins: Hmm. I bet he'll do it.
Me: Yes, he will. He'll do it because he'll understand there will be no arguing. You're being nice about it, and you're not leaving until he does. He'll also quickly realize that he looks like a jerk if he doesn't do it. He might gripe or stomp or sulk, but so what. When he's completed the task, you'll say, "Thanks," then take him to school.
Dad: I think I know what you're saying...
Mom: Do we do this every time?
Me: Some variation of it until he "gets it," and he will if you're

super consistent. You're simply creating a new arrangement in your parent-child relationship and a productive communication strategy—this way he'll have the opportunity to take care of chores and not be able to get upset with you.

Dad: And what if he doesn't do it?

Me: Then he'll lose all his devices the rest of the day, including TV. Just be concise and emotionally flat when you levy the consequence.

Mom: He'll be bored to death when he gets home from school if he loses his privileges.

Me: Good.

Mom: What if he says he'll do it when he gets home?

Me: Then let him, and he gets to have his stuff after he does it. Remember, you said you didn't care when he scoops—

Dad: And if he doesn't do it at all? I know we'll take his electronics. But what about the next time?

Me: You push restart. When he does complete the task, he gets his privileges back. You've started a trend of respectfully conveying, "What I say goes." You're the padded brick wall that won't hurt him when he runs into it, but he'll never be able to break it down.

This turned out well. The kid wasn't off the rails; he was just seeing what he could get away with and becoming more resentful towards his forceful and angry dad. Once the parents perceived their child through the correct lens, paid attention to their delivery, and worked on being consistent and Connected (not frustrated and commanding), the hard-headed kid became more responsible and respectful. Victory!

Sometimes a child can become a massive stinker at an earlier age. Let's say you have a seven-year-old daughter who is already starting to demonstrate some rigid-minded difficulties when she doesn't get her way. She's throwing a screaming fit in her room because she doesn't want to go to school (for whatever fake reason). You, being the individual with the most influence in her young life, are not getting upset—you are paying attention to your delivery and trying to help her figure out a few things, like: how to control emotions more effectively, meet responsibilities, and understand that arguing in this house doesn't work.

I'll do this example in list form. Here are the modern-day, constructive parenting action steps, because back in the old days, when things like this happened between a parent and child? Immediate corporal punishment. *Whack! Whack! Whack!* That's not good.

Tri-C mentality and course of action:

1. Everyone knows that going to school is a normal requirement.

2. No matter what she says or does, you can stay totally cool and not take anything she says personally because who knows what preposterous things might come out of that wily little mouth?

3. You respectfully and calmly say, "Hey, kiddo, enough. Let's get ready and go."

4. If that doesn't work, and she continues to act wacky and say ridiculous things, do not make it worse by locking horns with her. Say, "I love you, but we're not doing this. Whenever you're ready, I'll be in the kitchen waiting." Leave her room because you will not get sucked into the pageantry.

5. She will experience two different thoughts in her mind: A) I won. B) But crud, my parent isn't indulging me. She

might stay in her room, but if she follows you to continue her fruitless attempt to pick a fight, you act like an emotionless android, stop where you are, and stare at her with a blank expression. Why assume that stance? Because you've preprogrammed yourself to not get upset and you know this is just a game to play out. She has no power.

6. When she calms down (and she will), she can think clearly again. Eventually, she'll either tell you she wants to go, or she'll continue to stay in her room.

7. If you're a stay-at-home or work-from-home parent, you can wait her out and take her to school when she's ready. She will have no privileges in the meantime. If she's late to school, then she suffers a consequence when she gets home, but wait until she returns in the afternoon to deliver your penalty. If she "chooses" to not go to school at all, then (as mentioned above) she has no privileges all day. Nothing.

But here's the problematic part. What if you have to go to work or get your other kid(s) to school? Your obstinate seven-year-old *knows* the situation, *knows* you have other responsibilities, and *knows* she can't stay home alone. What I'm saying is, in the vast majority of circumstances like this, the kid capitulates and goes to school. However, if she absolutely refuses, then you manage your day just like you would if she woke up with the flu. She'll be totally miserable all day (not physically, and she might try to make you miserable, too) because she has no screens, no privileges, no nothing.

Tomorrow will come because it always does, and chances are she'll be fine going to school. You've won and successfully created a new precedent. The next time she considers being defiant or pulling something outlandish, she'll remember this experience, how respectful you were (i.e., your delivery), and how it did not work out in her favor. And it might take a few similar situations (which is normal), but most kids learn fast, especially when the effective lesson is always executed. Bring it every time.

Keeping your "you-know-what" together is a significant element of Tri-C that cannot be oversold. Stay as unmoved as you can rather than getting tricked into a heated argument or losing your mind. Otherwise, you'll provide your kid with more material to build the dreaded spite wedge you are about to discover.

The Spite Wedge and Magic Wand

> Hey everybody! Although we've already discussed a nice assortment of valuable Tri-C principles, I know it seems I'm mostly referencing how to best deal with various defiance issues. Nothing upsets adults more than when their kids aren't compliant, and when parents get upset instead of staying composed, the other parts of Tri-C fall apart. I've certainly got more general and important parenting fundamentals to cover as we progress, but allow me to periodically continue exploring other "difficult child" constructs during our Tri-C journey.

A common occurrence in my office is when traditional-minded parents bring their "I like to do things my way" kid because life at home is getting worse. A child who was a bit temperamental when younger has now become a moderately frustrated and confused adolescent. This budding teenager (or tween) who never seemed too deeply rooted in a surplus of empathy is feeling more formidable and trying to flex a growing, somewhat non-compromising agenda. The conventional parents are trying to force a circle into a square peg, which is the worst thing they can do. Parents push. The kid gets mad. Parents push harder. The kid becomes unmanageable.

The first time a child chooses to be disrespectful or test the waters and refuses to do what's asked, we parents naturally respond with some degree of firmness, such as, "Let me go ahead and make something perfectly clear: It is not a good idea to oppose me you little devil." But when our "employee" whom we can't fire ramps it up and demonstrates a pattern of unmistakable defiance, it becomes somewhat bewildering.

What happens, then? Angered parents take this relationship down the wrong path as tensions mount and life at home becomes a huge struggle. This is the creation of what I call the "spite wedge." Convincing a young human to want to mind continuously is hard enough without bitterness involved.

Here's another confusing thing: Why can a kid behave at school but act like a demon at home? Because school comes with structure, consistency, a clear hierarchy, and peer witnesses. The student knows that trying to get away with ludicrous behavior is out of the question due to hardened rules/consequences and potential ridicule from peers. However, at home, where it's safe and prohibited actions are "tolerated," mildly inappropriate behavior can eventually explode into over-the-top, farcical behavior. The gloves can come off completely. We parents definitely see the worst of our kids at home. (*And vice versa. Hmm.*)

Suppose an intrinsically willful child has become uncooperative and is now wanting to argue, throw tantrums (which we parents will never do because we're adults), or shut down rather than be agreeable. In that case, the newly built spite wedge acts as a juvenile barrier the kid embraces to keep the parents off-balance or prevent them from imposing more expectations. The young, unenlightened human will act in a passive-aggressive or very aggressive manner, and has yet to realize life is so much more pleasant when normal requirements are regularly met.

Parents are real-world agents who administer real-world expectations and can keep their kids from getting their way. Therefore, headstrong kids (who tend to experience more overall life challenges than their peers) can falsely blame or punish their parent(s) for all the consternation experienced both inside and outside the home. Unfortunately, home becomes a "safe" battleground, and the parents become the convenient targets because frustrated children often feel like they need a scapegoat or punching bag.

In the child's mind, it's easier to feel like the misunderstood kid with "mean parents." In order to fix this immature thinking, you can disassemble an unproductive home template, and rebuild a new, functional model. If "home is a microcosm of society," and you can ultimately create a productive and happy residence, the fruits of your labor will most likely result in a positive and responsible-acting kid who likes you, feels more self-confident, and operates successfully everywhere!

That's the spite wedge. And when an unpleasant encounter with a child starts to occur and the spite wedge needs to be dissolved before it can even begin, parents can refrain from any negative emotion throughout the interaction and execute a concise, distinct prescription. What's it called? The "magic wand."

Activate!

To commence, let's rehearse parts of Tri-C again. (*Fundamentals, fundamentals, fundamentals!*) We can look at the upset kid and the overall situation clearly and apply specific language to resolve the issue. Time for the Tri-C magic wand, where half the spell will be cast on you, and the other half on the child.

Remember, no matter how manipulative or what tactics your kid tries (I've had thousands of mini-lawyers in my office), understand that your child *knows* your ruling is fair but doesn't want to do it—do not think otherwise. Also, your kid might not want to mind you because of anger towards you for something you've said or done in the past (e.g., feelings of being unjustly punished, repeatedly critical of some type of performance like sports or grades). Because you may not even be aware of what it was, if you can stay composed and create a respectful conversation to explore the issue, it will help inspire your child to "melt the anger away" and not perceive you as the enemy, but see you as the caring parent—the way it's meant to be—with love and admiration. I've watched this positive shift transpire in my office countless times because the parent enacted Tri-C.

Let's reemphasize these procedural steps to sear them into your brain. In many situations, first ask *why* the defiant behavior or negative attitude is happening. Don't highlight your anger or the kid's actual behavior. Absorb this self-administered spell when your child is non-compliant, acting disrespectfully, or has broken a rule, as you might be inclined to get upset and make things worse. Note: Even naturally cooperative kids can sometimes appear argumentative—an occasional negative action does not necessarily indicate a spite wedge.

Regardless, the spell cast on you will remind you not to get agitated and **not to take what this kid says or does personally**. (I put that in bold for a reason.) The pure nature of effective parenting is a process that *must be played out fully*. With people, one thing leads to another leads to another—either a more positive or more negative set of actions will create a particular, everlasting outcome. Regarding the process of successful parenting, the arrangement of measures you execute calls for you to carry out Tri-C to its entirety. Only then will you achieve the concrete goal of helping the kid perpetually connect valuable dots without damaging your parental status.

If your child-rearing resume includes a history of hurtful interactions, your kid's spite wedge is most likely in full effect. You've made it easy for this child to be at DEFCON 1.

Listen, if your kid is coughing, you don't have to focus on the act of coughing. You'd want to focus on what is causing the cough. It's the same concept. Let's say your teen keeps choosing to say inappropriate things in the presence of the younger siblings. You can declare to yourself: *Let the Tri-C process begin.*

Instead of getting angry, start by mildly inquiring about "why" it's still happening. You take this calm approach because you're a mature adult who has all the power, and you know you have the means to fix this issue in a dignified way. You also know it's most likely happening because the immature adolescent thinks it's funny, wants to demonstrate some defiance, possibly reinforce the spite wedge, and get a rise out of you due to plausible built-up resentment (i.e., the negative elements which are the root of the cough).

After you casually ask the teenager "why" it's still going on, and your kid has no answer, you can say, "If you keep saying inappropriate things at home or to your siblings, you'll choose to lose your phone for the day." (Or whatever reasonable consequence you decide.) The young contestant might try to fortify the spite wedge with an attempted argument, but you're already done with this game show. And when I say done, I mean *done*. You do not have to continue the verbal exchange—and remember, it takes two to argue.

This parenting concept is also applicable if you've got more than one kid, because my guess is those siblings occasionally quarrel, which is normal. But if your children cross the line with each other, the same rules apply where you'll start it off with a conversation. But if/when the fighting cranks up to name-calling, inappropriate words exchanged, or physical violence, that calls for a strong warning. And when it happens again, a potent consequence.

Now let's say your teenager snuck out and you busted that desperado. This situation is a little more complex. What do you do? For this particular infraction, you don't have to waste much dialogue on the hazards of kids roaming the streets after dark. The young culprit already knew it was wrong and dangerous, so it would get maybe a 30-second review. The bulk of your approach doesn't have to be, "I can't believe you did that! You're in so much trouble!" (You would be focusing on the "cough.") Your objective is to cast a spell on yourself, get calm, and address the "cause of the cough" by non-condescendingly asking, "Why did you choose to do that?" (*Because it's fun and I hoped to get away with it.*)

This approach works magic in several ways. It eliminates potential friction that leads to arguments, more excuses, lies, or deflections, and the child knows it. *Ah, rats!* The kid thinks when the spell has been cast and a) it is time to accept responsibility for the chosen behavior, b) no spite wedge enhancement will take place tonight, and c) a consequence is coming that is well-deserved. You're also homing in on who the kid is (i.e., personal character) because by asking "why," you are taking a clear yet non-threatening approach of "this is not acceptable behavior" rather than "you will follow my rules or else!" In other words, you are addressing the source of the issue by helping the child take accountability instead of feeling defensive towards you. If you destructively yell and then punish, you're increasing the wedge the kid might want to reinforce. Down you go as you subvert your parenting, blow up the process, and make the child more difficult to deal with now and in the future. Agony.

"Why didn't you do your homework?"

If the oblivious or brooding youngster were honest, you would probably hear, "Because I didn't want to."

Instead, the response is nearly always some pathetic excuse or "I don't know," which then potentially leads to a squabble.

So if you disregard the magic wand, I'll have to smile and ask *you*, "Why are you arguing?"

Remember:

1. Your kid knows that always doing homework is a real-world requirement demonstrating responsible behavior.

2. All kids hate homework.

3. Arguments are ruinous to relationships. We do not have to argue. This is a Tri-C fundamental.

4. The parent is in charge, the kid has no power, and all parties understand this.

5. You genuinely want to know the reason and will address the kid's decision-making ability. You don't have to hammer the young human or emphasize the non-compliant behavior. If there is a valid reason or misunderstanding, then it becomes a conversation between the parent and child. No hurtful, false allegations are made. Always try to honor "blood is thicker than water." We parents can train ourselves not to jump to conclusions immediately, but instead allow the kid the chance to explain. People **hate** being falsely accused. Be patient during these conversations because the truth will almost always be revealed. If the truth is simply that your kid decided to be irresponsible, then appropriately address that.

If the parent instantly starts slinging indictments, the exchange goes down an entirely different avenue. The focus becomes the child's excuses or "symptoms" instead of the reason for the behavior. When we argue, we tend to get heated, and when we get heated, we say hurtful things, puncture the child's self-worth, and become controlling.

Those things injure the relationship, which is a direct violation of Tri-C. When the relationship takes on too much damage, the kid disrespects the adult. And when the kid loses respect for the parent, credibility disappears.

Whoops.

If the adult repeatedly gets outwardly upset at the child, the mom or dad cannot effectively uphold the two primary parental tasks—to protect and to develop—because the kid either becomes emotionally beaten down or doesn't care about what comes out of the parent's mouth. The spite wedge becomes bigger than the Great Wall of China.

If you choose to stay calm, back your kid into a soft corner, and earnestly ask "why" nearly every time a negative choice is made:

A) You won't get drawn into an argument.

B) The kid cannot justifiably get mad at you, perceive you as a threat, easily become defensive, and utilize the spite wedge.

C) You productively challenge the unfavorable behavior instead of getting too controlling, bossy, or irate.

D) The appropriate consequence (or briefly spoken reminder if the infraction wasn't too bad) will do the job.

Regarding more noteworthy transgressions which require a consequence, again, *the punishment will do the talking for you*. If the rightful consequence is painful enough, there is no legitimate reason for the parent to get angry or lecture and lose credibility.

For example, if you speed down the road and a police officer writes you a $300 ticket, the cop doesn't need to verbally lambast you—that would most likely agitate you and make you want to unjustifiably project some of the blame onto the officer and not accept full responsibility. It's just like what our kids do to us when we scold and continuously punish. Can you say, "spite wedge"? However, if the cop sincerely **asks why** you're speeding and acts courteously, it becomes difficult to deny responsibility—especially if you've already received a warning.

I know it's hard not to lash out and chastise our kids when they're provoking or annoying the snot out of us. If this is an area of potential cerebral rewiring for you, please be patient with yourself as you integrate Tri-C into your modus operandi. Learn to relax and trust that the rightful delivery of earned consequences—if it must come to that—will do the trick. Because a $300 ticket? Ouch. Back-to-back $300 tickets? Oh, man. Then another one? Holy cow. I am done speeding. Negative behavior ends. *Everyone gets it.*

If you're experiencing continuous non-compliance, try this respectful and effective style of interaction until your kid knows you mean business and grows in self-responsibility:

"Please take your laundry to your room when you get home—this is the third time I've asked."
Kid doesn't do it.
"Take your laundry to your room before you go to bed, please, or you'll lose your phone tomorrow."
Kid doesn't do it.
The next morning. "Well, you lost your phone for the day. Sorry."

And another:
"Can you do the dishes, please, before you go to practice?"
Kid doesn't do it.
"Hey, why weren't you able to do the dishes?"
"Uhh, well I uhh..."
(You can either allow one more chance—just one—or impose a consequence.)

Exchanges eventually evolve into examples like this:
It's a school day, and the kid knows exactly how much phone

time is allowed.
"How long have you been on your phone today?"
Kid looks it up, *deflates*, and hands it over.

These conversations represent a healthy model of learning for your child. Unmet expectations and breaking the rules warrant an exploratory conversation or warning, then an appropriate consequence if needed—just like if we get a speeding ticket for driving too fast.

I know most people like examples, so here's a longer one. This "effectively convincing the child to follow their rules" illustration demonstrates that the parents are more interested in maintaining a good relationship with their son than flaunting insensitive dominance:

A young teenager likes to ride his bike with his friends during the summer. They'll refreshingly go old school and cruise around, hit a park or two, play ball, visit different houses for lunch, play video games, etc. As this kid becomes more inconsistent with informing his folks of his whereabouts, the parents grow frustrated because they've already addressed this issue, and have asked him to be more communicative. The teen is cavalier about the whole thing which causes Mom and Dad to become even more flustered. These parents can either help build the spite wedge and give in to their anger—yell, lecture, and over-punish—or wave the magic wand.

> Mom: Why aren't you letting us know where you are? (Parents stay relaxed as they cast a spell on themselves and first ask "why.")
> Kid: Are you talking about yesterday?
> Mom: Yes. I didn't hear from you for four hours. You wouldn't respond to my calls and texts, and I've asked you to be better

about this.
Kid: We were playing a new video game at Jake's.
Dad: Did you not have your phone?
Kid: Uhh...I think it was dead. I was charging it in the other room.
Dad: It was also late. And getting dark outside. You know to be home before sunset, or at least check in and see if we're having dinner as a family. (Dad keeps it at volume "2"—no gasoline.)
Kid: Hmm. I guess I forgot.
Mom: Well, if you don't come home on time or let us know where you are, you'll choose to be grounded the next day. (Mom gives him the responsibility and sets a concrete, potential consequence.)
Kid: Okay. Sorry.

To summarize, the parents remained calm, didn't lecture, didn't go straight to punishment, and gave their kid the opportunity to demonstrate responsibility. These two adults worked as a team and created an appropriate condition where their son could choose his outcome. They also understood the importance of maintaining a unified parental front regarding all expectations, rewards, and consequences. If you're not sure you agree on an issue, go ahead and concur with the initial ruling, then you can discuss it behind closed doors if modification is needed.

Please do not undermine your partner, campaign to win favor, get in fights in the presence of your kid, or value one of your children over another. These horribly selfish actions all cause massive problems and are inexcusable. The child's well-being is completely violated by this immature, self-serving behavior which distorts the young, vulnerable human.

In the above example, the lazy parental response toward this young teen would have involved an exaggerated degree of displeasure. But, to reiterate, a somewhat willful child can get defensive easily and quickly lose sight of the parents justifiably being upset and trying to reinforce reasonable rules. The kid's focus becomes defending oneself instead of accepting responsibility, which then usually metastasizes into an argument, enhancing the spite wedge.

This is why I keep reiterating the value of parents looking at children realistically and not acting exasperated when their kids are doing something wrong. Kids will occasionally act wrong because young humans tend to test boundaries. This typically doesn't go over well with adults and can cause negative parental responses towards their children, which then causes negative feelings about themselves, and toward their parents. This is not a good cycle.

Here's a short and sweet example that demonstrates two different communication applications. Although it highlights a kid who is not exceptional in the cooperation department, these contrasting approaches and their effects (especially if exercised regularly) will significantly impact any child—either positively or negatively—depending on the parent(s) style of reacting:

A family is out to dinner. The tween daughter is hogging all the queso. The parents understand how she's genetically predisposed, but they also know that a part of her "knows better." The adults can respond in one of two ways:

1. "What is wrong with you?! Don't you think other people might want some?! Good grief!" This response creates indignation toward the parents and personal feelings of anger, embarrassment, and shame inside the kid. Damage all around.

2. "Hey, kiddo. Other people might want some." This response works: it snaps her out of her selfish mindset and helps the child stay in the reasonable part of her brain where she can work on how to jockey situations like this. No spite wedge, no false deflecting, and no shameful feelings created.

In the second option, the parents effectively check their daughter's behavior (and their rising irritation) and are "in cahoots" with her. Their positive focus is to help her learn how to independently operate more productively in society. In other words, they know she needs some guidance in creating appropriate social habits, and they understand this will naturally take some time, but she'll get there. The parents' determination lies in empowering her to develop mindfulness and to navigate life successfully—not impetuously get upset with her and contribute to her defensiveness or negative thoughts about herself.

As responsible parents, we'll undoubtedly have to issue disliked but necessary protocols (e.g., curfew, table manners, grades, screen time, chores) and firmly maintain them with respectful, non-spite wedge-building interactions. So remember, the parents' job is not to exercise dominance and force the kid to be compliant—their mission is to keep their eye on the prize of developing a child to becomes a well-functioning adult with strong self-esteem who has learned how to move through life successfully. *We have to embrace the long game of parenting.*

The Connected Way relationship and solid positioning of healthy standards help steer our kids from over-reactionary anger, help them gain the ability to meet real-world responsibilities, and keep them from constantly seeking cracks in the parenting wall because there aren't any and never will be again. If the parents choose to be inconsistent or disregard maintaining healthy family codes, they are welcoming one of the most powerful enemies of good child-rearing. Intermittent Reward.

Intermittent Reward

Stepping into the argument trap is way too easy. You might be growing weary of hearing this, but because arguing can be so destructive, even after becoming a Tri-C prescriber who knows to be respectful, avoid squabbles, keep your expectations realistic, and recognize that the consequences will do the talking, the need to try and convince our child to see things our way can be overpowering.

Throughout parenting, there's plenty of coaching involved. So when our kid demonstrates a lack of agreement, we feel the need to force compliance or educate (lecture) that person on why this reasonable standard is in place. *I must convince you to see the importance of this or the error of your ways* is our natural, parental instinct talking.

While we as parents understand that some things are negotiable, that exchange should *feel* different. Appropriate negotiations are positive relationship-building strategies. It's not about us when we're the ones showing flexibility.

We're *listening*. Hopefully our children feel comfortable enough to tell us what they want, need, and how they feel. It's up to us to foster respectful conversations and be super reasonable as to what is fair and healthy.

However, many humans like to tell other humans what to do. It's especially tempting when those humans are our kids. When a boundary is pushed and there is continued opposition? Oh boy, that makes patents nuts. Unfortunately, negative exchanges can spin into some nasty outcomes. What we want (expect) is for our children to quickly yield or admit the poor behavioral choice. How do we promote that? By eliminating the intermittent reward dynamic.

Intermittent reward (also known as Intermittent Reinforcement, developed by B.F. Skinner, the founder of Behaviorism) is widely regarded by psychology researchers as the most powerful form of motivation on the planet. It's why gambling can be so addictive. Gamblers hope that, despite the losses, they are destined to win at some point. When that finally happens, the thrill is so exhilarating it energizes another attempt.

Kids can fall victim to this addictive mindset when dealing with their folks. Their tireless determination can draw parents into a harmful argument where they grind them to a pulp and occasionally achieve success. We've all been there. And when we finally cave, we reinforce their desire to keep that strategy. Most children will push for nearly everything or try to get away with things until they realize they can't anymore. Why wouldn't they?

The parental goal is to heavily minimize that immature—yet—natural behavior, which is accomplished by being "the casino" where the kid does not win. If whatever wrongdoing happened because your kid chose not to meet a regular entrenched standard or is trying to push for something that will not serve in positive development, the young gambler should lose. Every time. Eventually, when the kid finally realizes there will be no wagering on this because of your unwavering consistency, the negative behavior will extinguish. But before the child realizes gambling (in this case, arguing) at the "parent's casino" is in vain, that card shark has to continuously lose over and over again.

"Okay, Brian, but my child is relentless. My kid will pressure me, try to grab my phone, start crying, scream, punch holes in the walls, and follow me as I try to escape. It's like I'm dealing with the Terminator! The kid won't stop!"

I know that sounds extreme, but for some of you it's a reality. Follow the Tri-C steps to eradicate that unrelenting behavior because when it finally ends for good, it's glorious.

Let's go through a few more examples so we know that you've got this. In each of these cases, both parent and child understand the expectation or consequence is fair and/or what the kid desires will not be granted. When your cunning high-stakes player begins the unsavory attempt:

Step 1: Relax.

Step 2: Get locked into the logical (non-emotional) part of your brain.

Step 3: Stay respectful and sheathe that power sword. Remember, this is a game and you both know who has the power. You are going to properly exercise your indisputable command.

Step 4: If a rule was broken, casually ask, "Why did you choose to do that?" (Cast the spell.)

Step 5: Although your child recognizes the direction you're taking the conversation, they will still try to argue, emotionally provoke you, or guilt you. Respond with something like, "I know you're bummed, but we've talked about this." No annoyance demonstrated by you because you don't have to act like that.

Depending on the emotional control skills of the kid, there are two different outcomes. The first few examples represent mild emotional intensity where the kid doesn't get too upset and succumbs without too much uproar. Later we'll do an example that demonstrates a more difficult affair. You also recognize that talk is cheap, so there will be no attempt from you to try to convince or lecture—you would be wasting your breath.

Note: As you try this on your own, don't forget to watch your delivery...

Example 1:
Kid: Yes, but Taylor had to take everyone else home, and I didn't want to be a jerk and say I had to go home first, and—
You, being very business-like: You know your curfew. You're an hour late and didn't even call or text me. You know the rules. You're grounded for the weekend.

Example 2:
Kid: Everyone else already has a phone, and I'm the only one who doesn't, and—
You: We've already talked about this. You get your phone this summer.
Kid: Yes, but...

Example 3:
Kid: Can't we please swim for five more minutes? Please? I don't see what the big deal is.
You: It's time to get out. Sorry.

From this point forward, a parent can choose to give no response (not another word, no matter what the child says or does) and, as we've discussed, sit there and stare at the youngster in total silence. An adult can stay unprovoked because we're talking about *a kid*, and a parent can train oneself not to provide *a kid* with any emotional power.

Let me include this new, satisfying feature that can be implemented if the child won't stop. You can reply with a very brief ender—something like the signature line from Kuill of *The Mandalorian*: "I have spoken." Or maybe from Pharaoh Rameses in *The Ten Commandments*, "So it shall be written, so it shall be done." You can choose to respond only once and zip your lip, or repeat the words every time your kid keeps grinding.

I know these lines are hokey, *but they work*. It's frustrating to a kid when a parent restates the emotionless phrase(s). The young human doesn't like it and wants it to stop. (Just repeating "I'm sorry" doesn't work. It's too palatable and comes across as a bit too gracious.) But the only way to get the parent to stop saying these irritating lines is for the child to quit asking or trying to argue. That's what we call "extinguishing the behavior."

It might take five to fifteen consecutive, separate situations to employ this satisfying tactic, but it will eventually sink in. The kid will not be able to hear those words any longer and will come to understand that you are not going to crumble. It's the same as going to the casino and playing slots on your favorite machine and losing money on every pull. Over and over and over. At some point, reality sets in, you can't take it any longer, and you quit. Maybe down the road you'll cross your fingers and give it a try for old time's sake, but guess what? You'll lose.

Be careful to use this response appropriately. If you go straight to it, that can be disrespectful. What I mean is, try not to state these lines as soon as your kid asks for something for the first time or when it's your child's first chance to explain behavior. Wait just a little to see if your child keeps trying to argue and isn't willing to accept your healthy parenting decision.

Also, be patient as you learn how to utilize this method. You will recognize when you're being baited, then something in your head will click—*Aha!* You will realize: *This is the part where I stop responding and stare at my kid like a robot, or repeat, "I have spoken."* Wow! It works!

Like this:
"Please, Mom? Let's go to Chick-fil-A. I'm starving! Please?!"
(This is the third time the kid has asked in less than 15 seconds, and the parent has twice given a solid reason why they will not go.)
"I have spoken."

"Please? I mean—"
"I have spoken."
"Why are you saying that?!"
(Coolheaded parent either says it again, or doesn't respond.)
Kid begrudgingly stops asking.

Another example:
"Why can't I spend the night at Lindsay's?" (This is the third time the kid has asked in 30 seconds, and the parent has already twice explained why the answer is no.)
"I have spoken."
"I haven't had a sleepover in forever! Please?"
"I have spoken."
"But, that's not fair!"
"So it shall be written, so it shall be done."
Kid stomps off, *will get over it*, and begins to perceive the parent as a composed, immovable force.

Here's a non-"I have spoken" situation wherein you've already extinguished intermittent reward:
You have a no-electronics-in-bedroom rule on school nights after 9:30 PM (because you're into healthy parenting). You catch your 14-year-old past bedtime with her phone at 11:00 PM (because she snuck it back into the room). You stand in the doorway and calmly say, "Why are you up, and why do you have your phone?" (Teens need a *minimum* of eight hours of sleep. Do not compromise on this. There is tons of current medical/psychological research on this topic.) Her excuses and harmless pleading hit you at a dizzying pace. However, you keep your cool and wait for her to stop, which she will because the magic wand has been cast on her. She ultimately remembers: You've previously issued a warning, you won't be drawn into a feud, and you won't allow her to turn this into something else.

You: Well, you lost your phone for tomorrow. Hand it over.

She sadly relinquishes her treasured device and thinks about how painful it will be the next day without it, but she recognizes how respectful you're being. Of course, she will occasionally break the rules—she's a kid. But let the consequence do the talking.

I encourage parents to always use their leverage when necessary, whether it's screen privileges, phone, car, or friends. I also remind them not to shame, patronize, criticize, condescend, say, "I'm disappointed in you," or be sarcastic. These negative communication techniques rip away at the Connected relationship. We are our child's hero, and heroes do not hurt their #1 fan. (*Our kid should think we're the bee's knees. If our kid doesn't fundamentally think that, then we're being inconsistent and unrelatable.*)

Unfortunately, with naturally uncooperative kids, sometimes their emotions can quickly escalate. Why? Three reasons. One, they're not getting what they want, and during this early phase of life, they still struggle with tempering that rigid-minded characteristic, which you are in the business of tackling with Tri-C. Although their intense feelings are real, the sooner you address this emotional and behavioral overreaction in their childhood, the faster it can be resolved.

If your kid is already a teenager, it is still fixable—it might take longer because the confrontational conduct has become more embedded. Tri-C effectiveness also depends on the level of the child's deep-seated emotional control—a bipolar or autistic youngster can struggle more to regulate emotions.

The second reason obdurate kids can emotionally skyrocket is that acting out seems acceptable, as much of their focus is narrowly placed on themselves. They can have difficulties recognizing how they impact others and the social importance of how they want others to perceive them. *But wait a minute.* Earlier, you discussed how certain kids could act totally appropriately at school but completely outrageously at home. How is that dichotomy possible?

This concept is very important to understand. Because deep down, they "do know" how to act, but at home feel like they can act out because they can get away with it. As mentioned earlier, lots of these intractable kids not only take out their frustrations at the house, but also don't feel compelled to act respectfully or with empathy at home. (*My parents have to love me no matter how uncooperative/disrespectful I am!*)

To revisit, empathy is being able to value what other people want and how they feel in their frame of reference. It serves as a governor to help suppress our self-centeredness. It also acts as a social supercharger that significantly helps bolster consideration toward others. We all "want what we want," but empathy allows us to set aside our wants because we value the relationship-factor more deeply.

Know that empathy is different from sympathy. Sympathy (compassion) is feeling sorry for someone, something, or a certain group, and feeling compassionate does not keep us from getting what we want (although it makes some people feel better about themselves). Strong-willed individuals can more easily feel sympathy than empathy.

Third, stubborn-minded kids want a sense of control (which they feel like they can occasionally fight for at home, in certain environments, or with certain people), and they want to be right. Unfortunately, inflexible kids tend to become irrational and can feel threatened quickly. They also try to prove the other person does not have unbridled authority which, of course, the parent does, and they know it. Administered correctly, Tri-C helps productively address these three issues.

Let's proceed to a more emotionally intense example not unlike some of you may have encountered. This involves "your" 16-year-old son:

Kid: I'm not cleaning my bathroom. I'm tired.
You: Come again?
Kid: I'm going to my girlfriend's.
You: You told me you would clean the bathroom before the weekend, and it's already Friday night. (You're setting the stage.)
Kid: Leave me alone. I'm sick of you.

Your natural instincts may have just shrieked at you to go off on this kid. But the reason your child is behaving like this is that he has some emotional/behavioral challenges—plain and simple—do not forget that. A naturally cooperative, mature-minded youngster hardly ever exhibits profound defiance or sheer insolence.

So here you are, getting into your Tri-C routine, keeping it together with the realization that you can exercise your patience with this child and play out this process fully, knowing ultimately you will be victorious.

Game time!
You: Not a good decision right there.
Kid: I can say whatever I want!
You: We don't yell and scream in this family. What's going on?
Kid: Why do you care?!
You: I care because I'm your parent.
(All you've done is set an awesome example. You've acted respectfully and tried to get him to holster those pistols.)
Kid: I'm not cleaning the stupid bathroom!
(Child is choosing to embrace his immature anger and digging in his heels.)
You: I'm sorry, son. You can choose to do it or lose your devices for the weekend. (Transactional, not emotional.)
Kid: What?! You can't take my PC! I built it!
You: I can and I will. And if I recall, I bought the parts.
Kid: I can't stand you!

At this point, the adolescent either storms off, blows up, or says something else inappropriate. You stay logical and do not respond. You've already made your ruling and won. Trying to reason with someone who is exceedingly defensive is almost as ludicrous as trying to reason with a drunk. *You know what? I think I'll just circle back when you're sober.* The child realizes you will not react to the drama and finally (hopefully) calls it a day. If it takes 30 minutes for this stand-up act to end, go microwave some popcorn. Again, you "have spoken."

Do not give in. Do not retaliate. You're following a course of action to create an everlasting, desired outcome. After your kid cools down (he will eventually move back to the reasonable part of the brain), you can conversationally discuss the unsuitable behavior and what he can do to help control that. You cannot allow unbound, unreasonable thinking and wild, inappropriate behavior to normalize. Ever.

Regardless of whether you have a productive conversation that day or the next, and he didn't clean the bathroom, all screens will be gonzo, including the phone. Tomorrow arrives, and your child wonders if you still mean what you said, until he realizes you've taken all the devices (unless he hands them over). You do not highlight the infraction or loss of privileges until that subject is broached *by the kid*. Trying to drive home a point or continuing to express your anger, as much as you might want to, infuriates that person and hurts the relationship. Let him sit in it. Your consequence will perform the assignment.

Realize, the less you talk, the fewer chances there are of exacerbating any issues. There is no reason to "add to" or argue. Stay unprovoked, and remember your kid already knows what the deal is and who is in charge—do not feel like you have to keep repeating yourself. Let me say that again: Stop talking. You've already said what you need to say.

You also understand how this young individual operates, so you know whether this artful dodger will try to find and/or sneak a device. Guess what? You're smarter and more determined than he is, and he won't be able to find any electronics. Take away power cords and turn off the Wi-Fi if necessary. He will either let it lie or ask you, "What the heck?"

To that, you will reply, "Because you didn't clean the bathroom, you chose to lose all your stuff for the weekend." Try not to ground or take privileges away for more than two weeks in nearly any situation. Two weeks is forever for a kid, and once you get past that marker, the punishment becomes monotonous, and you've lost what you were trying to accomplish. Don't forget to be specific regarding the consequences and the expiration date. Eliminate all ambiguity by avoiding disrespectful, autocratic responses like, "You'll get your phone back whenever I decide."

The child might mildly pop off, stomp back to his room, or raise another stink. If you kid freaks again, stay calm, remind yourself of the pledge you've made to the process, and see how far it goes. This might require much effort on your part, but typically the reaction will become less dramatic. He is beginning to realize that throwing tantrums is ineffective, you are a dealer who never loses, and he does not want another consequence issued.

And with that, the removal of intermittent reinforcement is underway! Keep in mind, the permanent end to this type of reward (i.e., the child "winning" in any fashion) totally depends on the parent's ability to stay reasonable, consistent, and undisturbed while delivering consequences. *Do not yell. Do not quarrel. Calmly administer an appropriate punishment.* Consistency is part of this process that parents seem to struggle with the most, but all parts must be fully enacted. Without consistency, there is no effective removal of anything. Inconsistency fuels intermittent reward. (*Boo!*) Consistency crushes it.

The steady application of Tri-C sends a very strong message: *Inmates do not run the asylum. I will not be threatened or bullied. I will not acknowledge your ridiculous behavior, and I will levy a consequence every time that is much more substantial than your choice to act rebelliously or not meet our normal expectations.*

Remember, the above example is a relatively drastic case. Based on your child's age, degree of immaturity, and willfulness, it may take up to six months (yes, half a year) before the child chooses to control emotions and recognizes that brazenly acting out is no longer worth it. But no matter the degree of severity, always stay on course *because this works.*

Unacceptable behavior and kids assuming any control can never be permitted. Home shouldn't be a chaotic madhouse, and the parent-child hierarchy cannot be allowed to shift the other way. You can never compromise on this. Kids do not know what they're doing regarding many things, and if your children somehow feel you are equals, or worse, "the boss," catastrophe follows. If you give them an inch, they will likely take a mile, and you'll have to work uphill.

Keep in mind, everything starts at home. You are teaching and modeling for your kids appropriate self-expression and to understand that screaming, bullying, and losing control will never get them what they want in life. The minute your children confront you and push a boundary, put a proper Tri-C stop to it.

This is important to keep in mind, so it bears repeating: Sometimes parents are doing a tremendous job administering the Tri-C philosophy for a length of time, and the kid is still regularly acting out of control, angry, disconnected, defiant, etc. When this happens it's time to make an appointment with a mental health professional or the pediatrician. There is likely something else at play, and pronounced behavioral issues can easily go from bad to worse if left untreated.

Effective Timeout: The termination of intermittent reward is also highly effective for little kids who can throw amazing fits when they want attention or don't get their way. How do we extinguish that? Step one: Remember that you are being reasonable when you say "no," and your children absolutely know you're being fair. Step two: Don't get upset. Go back to your brain training and don't take any of this seriously. We know lots of little tikes flip out until they learn that **does not work**.

Here's an example: You and the little one are outside playing, but now it's time to come in for lunch. Your kid doesn't want to and starts to resist. You ask or tell again. The tantrum starts, which means the child moves from the reasonable part of the brain to the limbic part, where it becomes very difficult to think reasonably.

First, you swiftly attempt to stop this cognitive shift by getting down on one knee and stating, "I know you want to stay outside and play with your friends, but it's time for lunch." *Respectfully.* The kid either moves back into the frontal lobe of logical reasoning and agrees (which happily becomes the standard once Tri-C is "The Standard") or doesn't and is now moving into full-blown, irrational overload. The child literally cannot think clearly at this point, so don't try to reason, force, beg, or argue because that ineffective approach **does not work**.

Since you're a mature adult who recognizes what's happening and knows how to proceed, quickly tell your child, "You can choose to come eat, or go to timeout." (Thank you very much, *Love and Logic.*) Sometimes the meltdown doesn't call for a consequence if it's not a broken rule, defiance issue, or a non-urgent situation—it's a matter of you ignoring the fit and walking away, as in *I will not indulge you, sorry kid*! For those types of tantrums, walk away every time or it will not stop.

Let's say your little one continues the fit and refuses to come in for lunch after you've asked again. You'll calmly respond, "I guess you're choosing to go to timeout." Point to a corner and see if the kid goes. If not, you can still pick up a small child (and you will) and carry that turkey to the designated area. You do not say a word. You do not act angry. Park that kid in the corner and walk away or sit directly across if you think the child won't stay.

Showdown!

What's going through the kid's mind is one thing, and one thing only: *This stinks! It didn't work! I want my way! Arggh!* But the child is also beginning to learn (keyword: beginning) that throwing a fit will not achieve what is desired, that you are the reasonable authority figure who will be in charge for 18 years, and that you will always expect and enforce appropriate behavior. After a minute or two, ask, "Are you ready to eat?" If the squirt says, "No!", you will say, "We'll just sit here until you're ready." And you will, staying silent, looking around, and being chill.

After another minute or two passes, ask again. What's now going through that little brain is: *This is not what I hoped for, and I'm not getting the reaction I expected, but I won't give in!* As the adult, you clearly comprehend this strategy and know you are more interested in doing what's necessary to end this type of conduct (forever) than losing your patience, so you stay on point and say non-condescendingly, "Let me know when you're ready, because I can sit here all day."

The kid is reluctantly starting to understand you mean business as you maintain your position, do not argue, and do not whip out the flamethrower. You are silent. You execute this process fully because you can outlast this kid in any predicament. Thankfully, the child will eventually shift back to the reasonable part of the brain and comply, leading us to talk more about consistency.

Consistency: I must revisit this with you, because when a child demonstrates any degree of unmet expectation, the parents must exercise an approach wherein consistency is an irreplaceable, top-tier principle. If you don't, and instead cave or scream or spank or argue, then not only will the child have to start all over—uggh, as inconsistency is the lifeblood of the deplorable intermittent reward—but also detrimental parental reactions will violate the Connected Way relationship approach, which we are now committed to upholding.

When various negative childhood behaviors emerge, Tri-C productively addresses and dethrones them. You might need to deliver a Tri-C strategy a solid five times in a row (it might take three, it might take twenty) to extinguish your child's irrational thoughts and negative actions. Your kid will learn that any oppositional conduct demonstrated will draw a sound response from you. **The most trusted sidekick of Tri-C is consistency.**

As loving parents, we can appropriately do what we must to foster positive behavior and steer our kids in the right direction. It is imperative for parents to painstakingly uphold normal family protocols. Earlier, I mentioned that children find cracks in the wall. If some healthy standards currently have some fractures (e.g., screen time, bedtime, disrespectful behavior), it's because the fervent young humans did a number on us and outmuscled us in the control department. Kids can develop the spite wedge and create land mines where parents become fearful to ask them to fulfill certain expectations. These scared adults tiptoe around, hoping not to upset their overly defensive youngster(s). You should never parent out of fear. When we do, we are being manipulated and have lost control. We must always work to be in control of ourselves and the situation.

As you unwaveringly administer the "end of intermittent reward" program and your respectful delivery of the "expectations will be met, I assure you" policy takes effect, the power will either remain with or shift back to its rightful owner: you. Tri-C is about appropriate control. We must have our kids' backs until they're old enough to have their own. And here's a great thing: once it has become abundantly clear that you run the show Tri-C style, you can begin to communicate in a more traditional, yet respectful, way.

Remember to watch your tone. (*Delivery! Fundamentals!*) Hard-headed kids tend to be sensitive as they struggle to interpret accurately all the layers of what is being communicated. If you do find yourself periodically using commanding verbiage (or sarcasm—that is a big no) because you tend to fall into the Compassionate Boss category, try to interact considerately and to not act put out; you are continuously convincing your children to accept your parenting and not begin construction on the spite wedge. "Me vs. You" is the diabolical saboteur of good parenting and can never become a theme.

Once you have devoutly implemented Tri-C for several months, your child feels remarkably positive toward you and understands that life is better when conditions are met. (Don't think you have to die on every hill—just 98% of them. Remember, some things are negotiable.) The child actually feels safe to *like* the parent. Deep down, a kid appreciates a caregiver who maintains healthy guardrails. It indicates the adult cares, which is fortifying and leads your young human to want to communicate more positively and consider what also is important to the parent.

"Hey, time for lunch."
"Okay."

"Can you scoop the dog poop?"
"Already did it."

And the child's intermittent reward career?
Terminated.

The Rhetorical Question and Follow-Up

Consider applying these parenting strategies to your regular dialogue. This is as important to remember as the multiplication tables in math. First, the rhetorical question: "Would you do me a favor and put up your shoes?" "What are your thoughts on helping me in the garage this Saturday?" "Would you mind keeping it down while I'm on the phone?" People appreciate being asked instead of told. Especially rigid-minded individuals who can misinterpret tone and actual meanings.

> Reminder: "Do I really have to do all that with my kids? I mean, my gosh. Shouldn't they just do what I say?"
> To that I reply, "Don't you speak respectfully to other humans when you want or need them to do things for you?"

It's also nice to include a window of time. "Before you go out with your friends, can you straighten your room?" "After you're done with your video game, would you feed the dog?" Parents who teach themselves to act kindly toward their kids have a much higher chance of getting their kids to regularly be agreeable. *Duh.*

Parents sometimes tell me they try the polite and timeframe approaches and declare they don't work. They're not successful because they won't consistently enact the follow-up. *All follow-ups must happen.* As we dig a little further into these conversations, parents admit this is where they mostly fail. They struggle in the consistency department because executing the follow-up creates more conflict (only at the beginning, until the kid knows the regulation will always be enforced), and/or because it's inconvenient. For instance, now the parents have to micromanage screen time, bedtime, or have a grumpy lout sulking around the house trying to make everyone else miserable. Or they must drive their teenager to high school. Or the frustrated parents "just don't want to mess with it." *Hello, intermittent reward.*

If I ask my kid to put away her backpack after she is done watching TV ("Hey, will you put your backpack in your room after your show?"), I know that won't necessarily be a top priority, so I'll keep my ears perked because I'm not exactly sure the task will be carried out. Once the program is over, I'll go to her and say, "Looks like that episode is done. Your backpack is waiting."

She says, "Hold on. I was going to watch one more. Can I do it after this?"

As the parent, we can look at the kid through the incorrect lens and get upset because we think this child should possess the priorities of a 20-year-old and "want to" perform this charge. Or, we can stay reserved, remember we're dealing with a kid, and tell her the time is now to fulfill the duty (or let her watch one more episode, then do it).

Regardless, if you're trying to break a chronic tendency of either innocuous or overt resistance, you can plainly state (you'll recognize this approach, and so will she): "If you don't put up your backpack, you'll choose to pay me five dollars." (Or some other appropriate consequence.) That's the follow-up. The super follow-up is when you make her pay because she actually left the scene and didn't do it.

To add to the police officer analogy, why would I stop speeding if I fly down the road and only receive warnings instead of tickets? Especially if I like to drive fast and I've got a shiny new Porsche. I will stop speeding when I get an expensive citation every time, or worse yet, if I lose my license for a while. Now that's painful. And I might not like to admit it, but I totally deserve it. *I'll finally stop speeding when I know I'm going to get a ticket, and, on top of that, I can't justifiably be angry at the nice cop. And on top of that, I might actually get to where I like the nice cop because the cop chooses to be so nice all the time. I have to stop speeding!*

The rhetorical question (and, when fitting, the inclusion of a timeframe) helps the youngster feel respected and feel there's some personal control over when the duty is executed. Successful child-rearing does not include "just letting things go" or exercising overwhelming dominance.

Sometimes, we see parents act bossy or disrespectful toward

their own kid when they're around other adults. *Look how much my child respects (fears) me, and see how high-powered I am. Or stop embarrassing me.*
"Sit up straight!"
"Go change clothes."
"What's wrong with you?"
"Because I said so!"
Uggh. So needless and immature.

In these situations, the misguided parents have emphasized *The Stanford Prison Experiment* syndrome (I'm in charge and it feels good to have this unquestionable power) or embraced their own wants or anxieties instead of their kid's development.

Development? Yes, indeed. As parents, we are always modeling behavior for our children. Our kids see and hear everything we do and take notes, from how we act around our friends to how we manage our time to how much we drink to how much we're on our phones! We demonstrate disrespectful communication skills if we constantly act high and mighty and with immunity. That's not healthy development. And if we spank our kids, we create two dreadful acts of harmful disservice.

Corporal Punishment: I won't spend a ton of time on this, but what I'm about to share is extremely important. We've still got some parents who physically discipline their kids. In 1998, the American Academy of Pediatrics (AAP) formally announced a recommendation discouraging parents from regularly spanking children as a method of punishment. In 2018, the AAP updated its policy and advised parents not to spank at all.

Hitting generates huge damage to the relationship. Huge. We do not like or trust people who strike us—I'm not sure how else I can state that. If we spank, we immediately take harshness and disconnect to an entirely different level, flushing the chance of a good relationship down the toilet.

Spanking also creates an endorsement of violence. I do recognize some kids can become so belligerent that a parent feels hitting is the only way to bring that individual back down to earth, get the kid's attention, or send an overpowering message that declares, "I am in charge and that behavior is not permitted." Please refrain from this form of punishment because it is so hurtful in so many ways.

I know this is a polarizing subject. Some of you may have a difficult youngster, and/or some of you possibly were parented this way. However, that does not make it right or necessary. I'm an old-school guy, but for parents to actually deliver a blow to their child because they are upset, trying to make a statement, or execute a punishment? That's rough. Tri-C is built in such a way that parents won't feel like that's a necessary option.

Timeout actually works remarkably well with little kids when enforced exactly as it's laid out in this book. If you have credibility as a parent and the situation (e.g., running into the street) calls for it, you can get eye-to-eye with that small child and give a powerful 20-second stern talk that will undeniably get your kid's attention.

So allow me to encourage you to remember the fundamental concept of continually motivating your children to relate to you and like you. Doing so includes healthy follow-ups but cannot include spanking. I want you to fully enjoy parenthood where your kids have the grand opportunity to benefit from how well you've fostered their positive development. It's the greatest thing ever when our children trust and enjoy us.

Partnering

People love to feel included in decision-making conversations, especially if it somehow personally involves them. It provides some ownership, which motivates them to want to fulfill the objective. Children greatly appreciate it when their parents are respectful and partner with them to solve certain issues, explore options, or create structure at home.

And for those of you who have black-and-white thinking kids, they seem to do better with steady structure and routine—it helps them compartmentalize their duties and not become overwhelmed with too many variables. (It also eliminates loopholes!) In essence, they feel more open to meeting responsibilities because there is a "comfortable" protocol to follow in their minds.

They also do much better when given a day's notice regarding certain upcoming situations because they can plan ahead (e.g., "When you get home from school tomorrow, remember, you've got tutoring for an hour."). In essence, partnering is an effective tool to teach self-responsibility and encourage cooperation—another win-win.

Let's discuss ways to partner with your kid. The rhetorical question and window of time strategies have partnership qualities, but those don't apply to all situations. Let's put school grades into play, as this is a common issue. Let's say a theme is developing where your seventh-grader is not doing an adequate job with academic performance. You naturally feel your frustration starting to emerge.

What are the parental options here? To scold, force, and punish? Sure, we can take that approach, but what does that get us? Nothing productive. Conversely, we can consider looking at the child through a clear lens and realistically determine what's the hurdle. *Why is this kid not doing better in school?* (Let me reiterate this: ADHD is real and a mighty foe of scholastic achievement. If your child is easily distracted, fights to do homework, and/or consistently misses assignments, is disorganized and impulsive, and struggles to focus on things that are not particularly enjoyable, i.e., school; please have this evaluated by a mental health professional or your pediatrician.)

As we now know, step one is to understand the actual reason for the issue. Then, we can influence the kid to connect the dots, and in this example, help the child realize (remember) that getting good grades is mega-important. Therefore, in true Tri-C form, first politely inquire "why" and see if there is a valid reason for the poor grades. By taking this approach, it helps the kid not feel defensive, but instead, feel like you're wanting to have a respectful discussion. Mature conversations help a kid learn how to fix things—lecturing does not.

If this situation boils down to simple immaturity (not a learning disability or overly difficult material), and if there is a window of time to play with (school is continuous, so there are many windows of opportunity), then we can partner with the child to create a workable solution. This kid—who never seemed to possess much of a sense of urgency—isn't "getting it." And if the parent tries to apply authoritarian force, that creates more problems. I don't think we're much interested in intensifying problems:

> You: What's going on with your schoolwork?
> Kid: What are you talking about?
> You: I looked online and saw some failing grades and missing assignments.
> Kid becoming defensive: I told you my teacher hadn't recorded them yet.
> You: Hold the phone there, sporty. I'm not mad. I'm just curious as to what's happening because I see a pattern here.
> (You won't get emotionally provoked—that way, you can try and disarm the child by approaching this as a discussion rather than a thumping. Plus, you've heard the lame "it's the teacher's fault" excuse before. Aim for brevity—try to avoid talking for more than 20 seconds at a time. This is an extremely important parenting strategy. If you go longer, you start preaching, which is not good. You can say everything you need in 20-second spurts, which helps the kid see it more like a conversation instead of being talked at. *I'll talk, you'll talk, I'll talk, you'll talk.)*
> Kid: Well, uh... (Excuse, fib, excuse, fib.)

You: Here's the thing. I don't care when you do your schoolwork (because you're not an overly controlling parent) as long as your grades are good and everything is turned in on time. How can this be fixed? (You are putting the responsibility on the child.)
Kid: Uh, I don't know.
You: Do you need me to help you in some way? I can go through your assignments with you and check your work.
Kid: No!
You: Whoa. Are you feeling okay? Is anything bad going on?
Kid: No, sorry. I just need to do it...
Parent: Okay, well, should you study and do homework as soon as you get home from school, or right before or after dinner?
Kid: After dinner.
You: That's fine, but sometimes we eat late because you have rehearsal.
Kid: On those days, I can do it earlier.
(What's happening is the child is coming to understand that living mostly in the fantasy world of "I'd rather blow off school" will not fly. An apathetic approach to academics is unacceptable. Because you're the adult, you'll be the one who will keep this exchange feeling conversational, and you'll adjust to find the correct broadband to communicate, prompting the kid to be more receptive.)
You: I'll leave it up to you, but you spend a lot of time on electronics, so here's what I think: On weekdays, you know you have only two hours of recreational screen time, so I need to do a better job enforcing that. We'll sit down together on Friday afternoons and go online and look at your grades. If everything is turned in and you're passing, then you'll get to have your phone, etc. for the weekend. But if there are missing or failing grades, no electronics again until Monday. (Concrete communication—no ambiguity, no room for loopholes, and what was said took less than 20 seconds.)

Kid: But it's going to take me more than a week to get my grades up and everything turned in and for my teacher to record it!
You: I'm not talking about checking this week. We'll look at next week.

As the parent, you have partnered by allowing your kid to choose when to do schoolwork. You have also upheld respectful dialogue and clear expectations by being transactional and conversational. It is now up to the student to choose to fix the grades. If your child effectively addresses the problem, that's great! But if not, let's see what happens next.

14 days later...

You: It's been two weeks, and zeros are still posted.
Kid: I'm trying!
You: Something isn't working. I don't see you spending much time doing homework.
Kid: Ugh. I'm just sick of school. And my teacher is a moron!
You: Because you chose to disregard school, there will be a consequence.
Kid: But that isn't fair!
You: So it shall be written, so it shall be done.
Kid: Can't I have another week? I mean—
You: I have spoken.
Kid: Oh my gosh! I hate it when you say that!
You: How about this? You've chosen to lose your electronics this weekend, but next week, with all grades passing and stuff turned in, we'll go out to dinner Friday after we check. (Reward: good) And remember, for your core classes, I'll pay you for A's at the end of the quarter because the world pays for A's. (More reward: good.) But if it still looks bad, you'll lose your privileges again.

The objective for this kid is to learn to be responsible with academics, and we do this by implementing a parenting strategy that creates the best chance for success. In a situation like this, it means watching your delivery and partnering to allow some decision-making ability regarding when to do homework and demonstrating accountability.

However, suppose you are being ultra-understanding and painfully consistent, and this approach still isn't working after a month, and it's not a learning disability (like ADHD). In that case, you might need to see if there's something else interfering—possibly the onset of adolescent depression or maybe some bullying. Also, I'm not so presumptuous as to tell you what your kid's grades need to be, but most parents are more satisfied with a hard-earned C than an easy A.

Let's run through a string of partnership examples:

Parent: You need a haircut.
Kid: It's my hair. I don't want to cut it.
Parent smiles: You look like a shaggy bum.
Kid: What's wrong with that?
(The parent knows how this nine-year-old is hardwired, so there is no surprise regarding the stubbornness; however, both parties know a haircut is imminent.)
Parent: I have an idea. Let's look online and see if there are some styles you might like.
Kid: Okay, I can do that.

We do not have to argue and instantly "force" our child to comply. We can get attuned to what works. Here's an example involving an 11-year-old daughter and her mother. Mom rocks it:

Kid: I don't want to play tennis anymore.
Parent, who already knew interest was strongly waning: What's happening?
Kid: I'm just tired of it. It's not fun.

Parent: Why isn't it fun?
Kid: I don't know. I've been playing since I was six. I'm just sick of it, I guess.
Parent: Then what do you want to do?
Kid: What do you mean?
Parent: I think we talked about you committing to the entire season.
Kid: I know. I thought I would still like it, but I don't.
Parent: Hmm. That stinks.
Kid: I'm just done.
Parent: Are you sure?
Kid: *Super done.*
Parent: You've got, like, eight weeks left? Can you make it?
Kid: I guess so. (The tween realized her mom meant what she'd said earlier about not quitting before the season ended.)
Parent: If you're not going to play tennis anymore, what do you want to do instead? (Parent was responsibly "developing" her daughter by requiring fulfillment of the commitment, then partnering with her to see if they could agree on a different activity.)
Kid: I can become a professional YouTuber.
Parent: Hmm. What else you got?
Kid: I knew you were going to say that. (Note: *The more predictable a parent is, the better. If you feel the need to be "unpredictable," save that for your friends as well.*) You mean like a sport or something, don't you?
Parent: That's exactly what I mean. Something physical.

After a few minutes, parent and child agreed to a return to dance—it was something she'd done back in elementary school, and now some of her good friends were doing it. But if she discovered it genuinely was not her thing once she'd given it an honest chance, she would have to find something else.

I had an old-fashioned dad in my office and his 10-year-old son. As much as he loved his child, he was having a horrible time with this kid's natural stubbornness. He told me he couldn't understand the concept of his son not consistently wanting to obey. (Obey? Were we talking about a dog?) Guess what that resulted in? Yelling. Lectures. Frustration. *Spite Wedge*.

I helped the dad understand it is *his job* to get his kid to be receptive to his parenting by waving the magic wand (Tri-C style: being relatable, asking why, staying considerate and patient, not getting frustrated), then partnering. After a session of covering the fundamentals, we went through a few partnership examples: "Which day would you like to vacuum your room?" "Do you want to take out the trash at night or in the morning?" Because the dad *embraced what worked*, the child instinctually shifted. He no longer felt like he had to defend himself; he felt like meeting his father's wishes! Respect leads to respect, which leads to easier parenting.

Here's another example. Mom is trying to determine what summer days her older kid must stay home next week to babysit the younger sibling. The parent could obviously tell the big brother the specific days he has to babysit, but she wants to show consideration:

Parent: I need you to stay home with your brother some this week.
Kid: Oh man, really? I already made plans.
Parent: Your grandmother is going out of town.
Kid: I thought you told me she was going to be here!
Parent: Sorry, things changed.
Kid: What about Molly? Can't she come to watch him?
Parent: Babysitters are expensive. Please help me out.
Kid: Okay. Which days? Derrick and I were supposed to play basketball tomorrow, and I wanted to see that new scary movie this week with some friends.

Parent: What's it rated?
Kid: PG-13.
Parent: Which day were you planning to go?
Kid: Probably Thursday.
Parent: So you want Molly here tomorrow and Thursday?
Kid: Can I check with Derrick first?
Parent: Sure, just let me know as soon as possible.
Kid: I'll ask him right now. Thanks Mom!

Easy and respectful. The kid knew the mom could have dictated when he would have to stay home or forced him to babysit every day. But the parent chose collaboration, which shows her respect for the relationship. This type of connected approach helps set an overall positive tone for the household.

Your child ultimately will follow your lead—your consistent, loving lead.

Some parents worry that taking a partnership approach weakens the parent-child order and that the young human—who naturally is designed to occasionally push the envelope—will try to take advantage of the situation and cross a "hierarchal boundary." When and if the kid does attempt to establish an air of equal footing by doing something like telling instead of asking, swearing at home, trying to inappropriately joke with parents like they're good buddies, or calling the parents by their first names, we can briskly end that baloney. Very respectfully issue a strong reminder; hopefully, that does the trick. And if not, then a legitimate threat of a consequence, or, an actual consequence if the kid doesn't fix it.

Feel free to occasionally sprinkle some humor throughout different areas of your parenting if you'd like, especially if you detect some potential contention brewing. That way you are still making your point while being pleasant, which persuades the kid to be less defensive/more receptive, and brings that child back down to earth.

I once heard a mom in my office respond to her eight-year-old who was becoming frustrated and complaining about consequences:

Kid: Why do I always have to do what you say?
Mom: Are my expectations fair?
Kid: Uh, I guess.
Mom: And if you're able to have fun and still do what's expected (Mom playfully pokes her kid's ribs and uses a funny voice), is life much better for you?
Kid, trying to act serious: Yeah.
Mom: How about (she throws her hand up and does a Hamlet impersonation), Yes, most honorable and perfect mother of all time.
Kid smiles and shakes her head: Yes.
Greatness.

Confident

If the kid you have raised for 18 to 19 years is genuinely confident, self-responsible, positive, has friends, forward-moving, has healthy coping mechanisms, and is well-adjusted, you have successfully completed your most important mission in life! There is no feeling more comforting than knowing the human you've shaped is headed to young adulthood as prepared as possible. Go ahead and pat yourself on the back because *you* played the premier role in this. And the fact that *Confident* is only one of five chapter headings in this book indicates how important this state of being is.

Let me tell you some reasons it's critical for humans to feel good about themselves. Self-confident and humble people enjoy life more, do not feel threatened easily, have better relationships, uphold healthy boundaries, conquer challenges, do not give up, don't depend on social media views/likes, and don't worship ridiculous influencers. They refrain from being needy and they strive for success. They're warm and affable. They don't take themselves too seriously, won't settle for mediocrity, nor do they make things about themselves because they don't have to.

Wait! I want to be like this!

Genuinely confident humans are heavily invested in life and the relationships they have with others. They get through the hard times and manage adversity as well as anybody. They accept responsibility, become leaders, do not make excuses, choose favorable ways to feel significant, advocate for themselves, and aren't co-dependent.

Kids raised constructively (Tri-C style) don't intentionally hurt themselves or other people, nor become warped souls who do crazy and demented things as teenagers or adults. (See: *Uvalde*.) Therefore, as the parent who has the most influence on your children's overall level of fortitude, you will always be asking yourself: *Am I currently interacting in a way that's either neutral or somehow advancing my kids' self-worth? Or am I... not?*

Confidence Killers

We all know that challenges loom for us parental units working to keep it together for nearly two decades to get our kids soundly equipped to the launchpad. For many of us, the hardest thing about parenting correctly is consistently overriding two things that make us human: 1) negative emotions, and 2) egoism, which states that deep down we are always motivated to fulfill our own self-interest.

Other people (including our children) can cause negative feelings. Regarding egoism, if we're driven to meet our wants and needs first, that particular human instinct can drastically hinder us from meeting others' essential needs, including our children's. In other words, to be an excellent parent, we must learn to control these powerful, innate characteristics. It can be extremely difficult.

We have discussed in great detail the harm of feeling unfavorably toward our children, and we've also mentioned how human selfishness keeps us from effectively enacting the two primary parental tasks: to appropriately protect and develop. If we allow our negative feelings to be a significant player, we contaminate the crucial relationship upon which all good parenting is built, because we now know our kids *must like us.*

If we are unable to meet our children's needs over our wants and needs, then we cannot adequately protect and successfully advance our kids; thus, they will run into enormous developmental trouble. Again, the first 18 years of life are all about development, and as humans travel through childhood and adolescence, we need to be guided by self-assurance, not polluted with self-doubt.

Egoism might be the biggest personal hurdle to deal with as a parent. To effectively regulate it, a pronounced shift—what we earlier called "mental recalibration"—must occur in the adult's mind. It's the transition from an innate, selfish way of operating, to a selfless, "What does my child actually need from me right now?" overriding system. When and if the parent commits and legitimately makes the conversion, that's the game-changer. It leads to the sweet spot of successful parenting.

To refresh, the sweet spot is managing the kid—which includes control—while maintaining a great connection. And because feeling controlled is an ideal way to sabotage any relationship, good parenting can be perceived as though it's almost designed to fail. Luckily, Tri-C provides the winning playbook.

What all kids ultimately require is orthodox: parents' love, acceptance, and approval with no conditions attached. This essentially means: *I will always work to interact with you respectfully—no matter what you're doing—and I will always love you, and you know it.* If we do not make that a well-established principle, then we're forcing our children to deal with a litany of problems. Initially, kids perceive their parents as demigods. If those mighty figures interact harshly/disrespectfully/dismissively towards their naive children throughout the early years, then those little people assume the problem lies within themselves, since the formidable caregiver(s) most certainly cannot be at fault.

How many times have we seen a mom or dad painfully rip into their small kids while shopping? With a vicious sneer and such cruel words you'd think the parent was going to pull their little heads off. Self-confidence comes from within, and parents influence how lots of things materialize inside their children. Our kids are always looking to us for love, guidance, and acceptance. The parent(s) mentioned above are acting insufferably immature and cultivating fear, shame, belittlement, and disparagement. That type of approach makes kids feel terrible about themselves! Executing a destructive instead of constructive way to shape behavior is crushing, tearing away at children's self-worth. Very sad.

I hear certain parents ask, "Then what am I supposed to do at the grocery store when my kids are acting out of control?"

I respond, "Is 'out of control' the correct term? Or are they just acting like children their age being a bit zany in a stimulating environment?"

"Uhh, well..."

I continue, "If you're already a Connected parent (and everything positive that means), then you talk with them respectfully and encourage them to act cooler, and they will because you have credibility. They like you and don't want to upset you. Plus, they know they're being kooky and will receive a consequence. If you're not a Connected parent (yet), then you start the Tri-C process." Take a breath. Deescalate your emotions. Get logical. *Follow the formula.*

I once read an article that declared most parenting books create more anxiety. I assume that's because many are not good. Tri-C is here to help you comfortably follow an authentic roadmap of productive child-rearing. Believe it or not, I've watched certain parents get Tri-C up and running effectively, but they get lazy and/or disturbingly long for the exercise of gross power and resort back to insolent control. I know, I can't believe it either.

But for those of us who are normal, let's begin the "building confidence in our kids" discussion with a common parenting *faux pas*: telling our children how they "should" think or feel about things. No one has the right to dictate that. For example, "Oh come on—I know you like being in band." Or, "I can't believe you're so upset about that!" Or, "What's wrong with you? Don't you like to trick-or-treat?" (I'm relatively certain none of us have ever said things like that.)

Instead, we can act patiently, minimize our parental anxiety, and issue a response that allows the kiddo to work out the issue. "What's going on with band?" Or, "You seem upset." Or, "What do you want to do about Halloween?" This might be a hard habit to break, but we must try.

How? We can listen to our kid, take a minute to show respect through a conversation instead of immediately dictating how *we believe* our child should feel, and help that young person create independent solutions. In other words, we can slow down and try to talk it through like the earlier example in Chapter 3 of the daughter wanting to quit tennis. The mom could have thoughtlessly spouted, "What are you talking about? You like tennis! You're good at it, and think of all the money we've spent on lessons!" But instead, this mother treated her with dignity, investigated the issue, determined her kid was clearly done with that sport, and partnered with her to create another healthy option. This met the parental goal: to appropriately develop her child. This parent set aside her own wants and placed the priority on her child's healthy growth.

This tactic is hard to execute consistently because we parents either get self-important, or feel like we're in a hurry. *I don't want to have to stop and think: Okay, hold on. What's the best way for me to respond to my child who, for some reason, doesn't seem to want to do this, especially when I know what's best. (I, I, I...)*

Will most of us likely have to train ourselves to recognize when we do this? Yes. Will we have to consciously break the bad habit of inconsiderately just "telling" our child how to think or feel? Yes. But when we start to experience quality results (i.e., our kid becoming more mature, self-responsible, and courageous), it positively energizes us to continue the effective interaction. We can coach ourselves to recognize these situations, tap the brakes and listen, and employ the productive script.

I know most parents who administer the "here's how you should feel" controlling technique are not doing it maliciously, but if we're going to be honest, it's shaming and manipulative. Also, realize if a person is constantly told one's own thoughts/actions/feelings are not "right," then something must be wrong, and self-acceptance is torpedoed.

> **One cannot feel confident without self-acceptance, as everything in our lives is based on how we feel about ourselves. Everything.**

If tactless messages from the parent are infused with either blatant or underlying disapproval (or any of the other shoddy parenting aspects we've discussed), then the skewed child spends a needless amount of energy to try to overcome the negative effects. The goal is to provide a home environment where the child can work on self-awareness, self-identity, character, and grit, which means you act like a rock-solid adult who stays understanding and always puts your kid's needs over your wants. Your daily communication strategies can create a landscape of healthy self-growth or chronic self-uncertainty.

How about a few helpful examples:

Child: I don't want to go down the slide.
Parent: What do you mean? It's fun! All the other kids are doing it. Are you a scaredy cat?
(WRONG)

Child: I don't want to go down the slide.
Parent: What's up?
Child: I don't know. It looks scary.
Parent: You want to watch for a while? Or try it once and see how it goes?
(CORRECT)

The young human doesn't feel forced or shamed and likes the parent even more. Chances are extremely good the kid is going to hit that big slide sooner than later (give it a minute, or the next outing), especially after being allowed the opportunity to develop the courage to do it independently. Now that's powerful.

Child: Hey dad! Want to come look at my dress for the fifth grade dance?
Parent, who is tired and just got home and wants to sit on the couch and scroll: I don't think so, maybe later.
(WRONG)
The young daughter feels unimportant and discounted by her superhero.

Child: Hey dad! Want to come look at my dress for the fifth grade dance?
Parent, who is tired and just got home and wants to sit on the couch and scroll: Of course! Wow; you're going to look beautiful!
(CORRECT)
The dad made sure his kid knew she was priority #1.

Child: I hate school.
Parent: No you don't. Think of how much you're learning, and...
(WRONG)

Child: I hate school.
Parent: Yeah, school can be tough sometimes.
(CORRECT)
Most kids don't really like school; chances are you didn't much either. Children know they have to go, and they know they are expected to do well, that's been made very clear. We don't have

to try to encourage/force them to like something that isn't relatively enjoyable. Our kids appreciate us as parents when we act empathic instead of presumptuous. Believe it or not, strategic parental responses like this typically motivate kids to be more responsible because they see us aligning with them and not being commanding. We're building relatability instead of resentment.

Child: I'm sad.
Parent: No, you're not. You're just saying that because—
(WRONG)

Child: I'm sad.
Parent: Why is that?
Child: Because Jenny's boyfriend broke up with her.
Parent: Aww. That is sad.
Child: I feel sorry for her.
Parent: You're a great friend. What do you think she needs from you?
Child: Hmm. To be there for her?
Parent: That sounds good to me!
(CORRECT)

As mentioned earlier, a kid can't handle frosty dismissal or the sinister bombardment of criticism. To develop properly, the child needs the exact opposite. Not: *Meh. You're nothing but a kid. I can say whatever I want, and how you feel is irrelevant. Maybe you'll stop acting that way if I shame, criticize, or guilt you.*

Why didn't you catch that?
(WRONG)
Almost. Here comes another one.
(CORRECT)

Seriously? Are you kidding me?
(WRONG)
Hey kid. What happened there?
(CORRECT)

You'll never get it.
(WRONG)
Let's keep going.
(CORRECT)

Countless sessions in my office involve me attempting to convince the parent(s) to realize that nearly every trying encounter with their kid can be either positive or neutral, rather than negative and Directive. It's the best thing to experience when parents set aside their own issues and take appropriate command of the job they signed up for. Because when selfishness, laziness, arrogance, frustration, or anxiety are allowed to become the parents' puppet masters, the child suffers. What an avoidable shame.

Anxiety: Because I'm a clinician who understands the rampant nature of anxiety and the gravity of its negative effects, parents need to be privy to this information. There's a decent chance one of your kids might be afflicted with it. (Anxiety and stress go hand in hand, so we'll discuss stress in the next chapter.)

Anxiety is the heavyweight champion of all mental issues. The National Alliance on Mental Illness and the National Institute of Mental Health report more people struggle with anxiety than all other diagnoses. Regarding self-confidence, it's the Mike Tyson beat-down of all behavioral health beat-downs.

I've treated numerous kids with anxiety who look great on paper: smart, nice-looking, creative, personable, athletic, good family, etc., but their self-esteem is in the toilet. Why? Because as anxiety goes up, confidence goes down. Let me explain: Humans are not necessarily in control of what goes on around us; therefore, we need to be in control of what goes on inside us, meaning our thoughts and feelings. Our thoughts (the ones that require our focus) must be rational, pragmatic, and controllable, and we need to be able to regulate our emotions effectively.

Pronounced anxiety almost always starts right out of the gate at birth and can grow from mild/manageable to severe by late adolescence. It comes in a wide variety of symptoms, which means it can be impactful in many different ways. If someone chronically second guesses oneself, overthinks certain issues all the time, or if too many irrational cognitions are constantly distorting thoughts and grinding down the individual, then that person feels exhausted and out of control. If a person regularly feels out of control, self-doubt becomes a significant player. That individual, unfortunately, begins to dwell on difficulties and over-amplify troubles. That is not a healthy mental terrain for self-confidence, which should be loaded with stability, self-assurance, and rational perceptions of self and the world. Thoughts need to be accurately processed so functioning can be normal.

Clinical anxiety tends to increase as children age, and humans develop coping mechanisms to deal with their issues because we hate to feel anxious. Sometimes kids' coping mechanisms are harmful (e.g., self-injury, eating disorders, drug/alcohol abuse, reckless behavior), and the more dysfunctional behaviors run the show, the more acceptable it becomes to get out of control. It is never permissible to normalize dysfunctional behavior. Anxiety and negative actions can also lead to depressive symptoms. Do not hesitate to seek professional help if your kid's problems can't be resolved at home. Untreated anxiety has ruined too many lives.

I will always suggest finding outside help when you see something is profoundly troubling your child, for two big reasons. First, unless you're a mental health professional, you're not trained to effectively address an out-of-the-ordinary behavioral issue, just like when your kid has a terrible respiratory infection, you look to a doctor to treat it. Second, because you are the parent, your child needs you to be assertive and find appropriate help when serious problems arise. Various problems commonly develop because we are humans, and unfortunate things can happen along the way.

Acceptance and Electronics

Note: What you're about to read lends itself to dealing with today's technology-heavy world. How well you manage and enforce the following concepts will significantly impact your kid(s).

Let's look at what may seem to be an odd pairing in the confidence-building department: acceptance and electronics. We've got two primary parts regarding acceptance: 1) From parents, and 2) from peers. Both are huge. Clearly, it begins with parents. We've discussed the value of parental acceptance of the child, so let's talk about peers.

Kids need friends and face-to-face social interactions. This is irreplaceable. For extroverted youngsters who possess strong social skills, this task is relatively easy to meet. There is an internal force pressing outgoing individuals to interact more fully. The more we engage in something and the more practice we get, the more masterful we become. This is true for making real friends and connecting with others. However, kids who tend to be more introverted or lacking in interpersonal skills absolutely must have social repetition. For shy or quirky children, electronic devices have become public enemy number one.

I'm not saying that the internet and all things digital are bad. Technology is necessary and can be great. Unfortunately, we have provided our youth with a medium that can be too big for them and has become beyond captivating. How can we expect our children to be responsible in the digital arena when there are countless adults who cannot effectively manage it?

Some of you will *love this*: I highly encourage no fixed devices in kids' bedrooms, primarily televisions and desktops. It is too difficult to oversee what they're viewing/playing and their actual time spent looking at a screen. I assume a number of parents already have allowed a TV or PC in their children's rooms. The easy thing would be to ignore my suggestion.

So how about this:

Mom: Hey kid, I hate to tell ya, but your dad and I have been talking, and we feel it's not a good idea for you to have a TV (and/or desktop) in your room.
Kid: What?!
Mom: I know. Sorry about that. We should've never allowed it in the first place.
Kid: But I need it!
Mom: Actually, you don't. We can set up your computer in the "whichever" room, and you can play video games or watch TV in the "whichever" area.
Kid: But why?! Things are fine!
Mom: Because we can't monitor what you're doing or how much time you're spending staring at a screen.
(This is the part where the kid knows the parent is right. This cannot become a debate that goes back and forth because this young litigator will say anything to win.)
Kid: But that's not fair! All my friends have a TV in their rooms! It's not hurting anything!

If this example represents how this might go down in your house, the hardest element will be to not lecture or get drawn into a clash. If you've already been implementing Tri-C at home, your kid will recognize that arguments are no longer a thing and will more quickly submit to your responsible ruling. It might take a week or a month before your child gets over it and adjusts—which inevitably will happen—and understands you were justified in this healthy protocol. If you need a quick "how not to argue" review, don't sweat it; go back to Chapter 3 and look under the *Intermittent Reward* heading.

Children can expose themselves to inappropriate material (including certain video games) and navigate through online milieus they are not mature enough to handle, including pornography and various social media apps which can suck them down into a hypnotic, overly-stimulating hole and expose them to disturbing, toxic images/messages. Keep a heavy finger on the pulse of your kid's level of electronic engagement—I've heard horror stories that were generated through digital communication (e.g., sending nudes, threatening suicide for attention, middle school kids having sex, boastful videos of drug use, etc.)

The world of electronics and social media provides too many corruptive opportunities for kids who are literally left to their own devices. Get educated on the potential for danger. Ask around and do some research to see what the most current, positive-reviewed parental apps and software are available to help you provide adequate safety.

Kids will always be mean to each other, but holy cow, the internet has created an entirely new phenomenon. People can hide behind their screens and communicate in ways they never would face to face. Children can become victims of virtual bullying and harmful interactions (e.g., feeling threatened, left out, less than, high-risk peer pressure). I've worked with responsible parents who tell me they've uncovered things their kids have been engaged in and viewed, and some of it is awful.

Many parents also are guilty of simply permitting way too much screen time (including phones, *"My Precious!"*) that lures kids into the electronic world to utterly disappear. Unfortunately, this prevents children from important opportunities to develop the social and life skills they so desperately need. Interacting virtually does have value, but it can't replace the worth of consistently being in the actual presence of others as one learns to build deep, meaningful friendships, receive critical feedback, experience the physical world, and deal with all kinds of people in all types of face-to-face situations.

Dr. Albert Mehrabian led one of the most well-known research projects on nonverbal communication in the 1960s. He concluded that the interpretation of a message is 7% verbal, 38% "tone/delivery," and 55% visual. That means 93% of communication is nonverbal in nature, which in today's world translates to: *I'm going to align with and understand you much better if we can interact with the 3-D versions of one another.*

There's a strong argument that a considerable amount of human success in life hinges on the ability to relate well to other people and become well-rounded. Therefore, letting children spend an inordinate amount of time glued to a screen harms personal development, violating one of the primary parental tasks. In other words, as parents, we must limit our kids' time on devices, help them pursue worthwhile personal interests, and dutifully police what's being viewed, particularly social media. When we were little kids, our folks did not let us watch R-rated movies/shows on cable (and we shouldn't let ours, and you **know this**) or sit in front of the TV all day and night, even though many of us tried.

"I'm bored" our kids will moan after their allotted screen time is up. Tell them to grab a broom and watch them miraculously find something else to do. It is not your job to *entertain* your children, especially once they're past third or fourth grade. It's okay to partner with your kids to generate some options, but don't feel like it is your complete responsibility. They will find things to do—maybe even with family! Hopefully, a decent amount of their affairs will happen with "real-life" people, like in sports, dance, music, art, or even cruising around the neighborhood. Older teens probably need to get a job (especially in the summer) if they aren't involved in hyper-competitive sports or activities.

There's tremendous value in participating in sports or competitive extracurriculars. Your children do not have to be all-world at whatever they're engaged in, but we learn so much about ourselves and life through competition. This is not limited to athletics; there is competition in art, theater, music, etc. Identify your child's strengths and interests and diligently explore them. For real, laziness be condemned.

When parents allow their kids to spend most of their free time staring at a screen, they are robbing their children of the chance to build fulfilling, substantial lives. I'm painfully passionate about this. I've seen too many kids in my office whose parents have sabotaged their children's crucial growth by not taking technology seriously.

The more humans work to get good at something considerable, the better we feel about ourselves and the more of a healthy identity we create. Kids (especially teens, as we've discussed) are always working to define themselves—it is a developmental fact. The goal is for a fair share of their effort to be devoted to enhancing their personal strengths, not being subjected to honoring their personal shortcomings, which unfortunately happens more easily if they're chronically locked onto a screen and not allowed enough formidable energy/experiences to flow through their souls and build them up.

You want them to explore potential positive identities:
"I'm a musician."
"I'm a soccer player."
"I'm an actor."

Versus:

"I'm not good at anything."
"I'm a nobody."

"I'm sort of good at the piano, but not really. I just play video games and watch YouTube all day."

The holy trinity of self-regulated wellness (which also seriously plays into our mental health) is **adequate sleep, a healthy diet, and regular exercise**. As responsible parents, we cannot compromise on upholding the primary parental tasks. Not everyone is an athlete, but we can make sure our kids stay physically active. We can also be diligent about our children's diet and manage their sleep schedules, especially during the school year.

We have 18 years to try to appropriately condition our kids to become self-responsible and hope our influence was effectively delivered; they are not supposed to condition us. Our children's "North Star" should not be the virtual world. It should ultimately be honoring themselves where they don't "need" too much of anything or anybody to feel happy or adequate, especially as they move into the young adult world. We want our kids to be able to reach their maximum potentials, which means throughout upbringing, they've got to have and want legitimate opportunities in the physical/real world to positively develop strong senses of self-worth and self-competency.

This is where our dedication to consistency comes into play. Good parenting can sometimes seem exhausting, but we signed up for this. Responsible parenting calls for us to be more relentless than the sedentary, device-loving youngster who can dig in and fight like mad for unlimited screen time and a lazy lifestyle.

If your kid is talented at a sport or a competitive physical pastime, great! Hopefully the child is active, developing a healthy identity, interacting with other kids, and learning self-discipline, teamwork, how to graciously win and how to deal with defeat—all well-rounded life skills that help build self-confidence.

But when a kid isn't athletic, it's still critical for the child to be involved in something physical or outdoors (e.g., martial arts, weight training, climbing, biking, hunting, fishing) while actively competing in some medium, physical or not. This goes hand-in-hand with limited screen time. Options abound when electronic ecstasy is appropriately tempered and not used as a convenient babysitter or as the primary source of engagement.

As alluded to earlier, two to three hours of **recreational** screen time on school days (depending on the kid's age and all responsibilities being met), along with four to six hours a day on weekends (unless it's a special occasion or a creative project) is very reasonable and will certainly prompt the young individual to find other things to do. Four to six hours on a Saturday or Sunday may sound excessive, but if your child sleeps eight to ten hours, that still leaves lots of time for non-electronic activities. Let the kid decide how to spend fun screen time (e.g., three hours on Play Station and two hours on the laptop).

Realize you'll probably have to *heavily* police time spent online until your kid potentially demonstrates some self-responsibility. This might sound draining, but consistency and commitment are irreplaceable anchors of good parenting. You'll create a screen time culture for your household, where it will either be a counterproductive "all day every day" electronic free-for-all, or you're the digital device patrol (in some capacity) for 18 years. The approach you take will unquestionably impact the outcome of your child.

I've treated a number of kids who've temporarily lost their technology privileges due to some infraction. The parents then tell me how much more "normally" and pleasantly their child is acting. What has transpired is that the kid is not suffering from online intoxication and understands there is no seductive, farcical virtual world to plummet into where it's stimulating, fun, and easy to disregard expectations. The child now has invaluable opportunities to personally interact with others in the real world, develop useful areas of functioning, and be more open to meeting real-world requirements. Kids can adjust to nearly anything when they have to, and for lots of families, making the adjustment to less screen time is the most important move that parents can make.

Allowing too much screen time (including phone) also prevents our kids from effectively growing their full imagination and creativity. The virtual world is too enticing and they get instantly sucked in, hour after hour, day after day, and experience unnatural, chronic dopamine rushes from the bombardment of irresistible digital stimulation. *"My child has the attention span of a gnat! I can't even get this kid to play a board game or sit through an awesome, classic movie!"* The shallow fulfillment provided by online activity has addictive properties, enticing children to continually be reabsorbed and experience harmful, mind-numbing highs and lies instead of actively participating in real-world, meaningful ventures and developing important skill sets and creative outlets.

Too much personal screen time is destructive to our children's well-being.

Limiting technology has two powerful confidence-building elements. One, you generate the mandatory time your child needs to broaden and strengthen other areas of life. Two, because humans are a herding species and require meaningful relationships with others (three-dimensional, not just two-dimensional), your child's social skills will likely advance because the kid is forced to connect with others offline. If the most attractive human characteristic is confidence, your kid feels more self-assured as personal strengths and social dexterity are afforded time to mature. This will impress some peers. You think your kid is great, and your kid will have real friends who feel the same.

Although your child will certainly run up against some bullies (physical and virtual) and other tough players along the way, steady, in-person social interaction will help create a friend group (small, medium, or large—depending on how introverted or extraverted the kid is) to hang with and help feel accepted, develop richness in life, learn about self and others more intimately, and provide important peer support whenever needed. A kid must feel liked and accepted by some peers. If your child is 10 years old or older and does not seem to have at least a few good buddies, investigate that. Identify what type of young human you've got, locate your kid's tribe, and create opportunities for your child to cultivate in-person friendships.

I cannot put a high enough price tag on how important it is to have real friends and diversified strengths and interests. For those of you with a somewhat introverted/eccentric child, get ready for that banshee to howl when you limit time on devices and press for more healthy engagements. But unless you uphold hard protocols regarding technology, a reserved kid who lacks self-initiative can completely submerge into social media, watching videos, the computer, a smartphone, and/or video games if allowed.

And speaking of introverted, reserved kids usually need a little decompression time when they get home from school, especially after having to interact with multitudes of people all day. Let them chill for a bit before you flood them with questions or chores—they're probably a little worn out. However, you may need to monitor their screen time as they recharge.

Quick suggestion: No phones at the dinner table or when you're out to eat, and this applies to *all* family members. Remember, your kids are always watching how you operate, and they're more important than whatever is happening on your phone.

Again, the key is "appropriate" time spent. You are trying to help your child achieve some balance. As crazy as this sounds (but maybe not so crazy), minimizing screen time might be one of your greatest challenges as a parent.

Trust

Because you are the most powerful, influential figure in your children's lives, demonstrating you trust your kids helps promote confidence like nothing else. You're sending the message that you're convinced they can handle the age-appropriate situation, and you trust good decisions will be made overall. Lots of kids appreciate being given responsibility—they don't want to mess it up and want to prove to the parent(s) they can handle whatever it is.

Some parents have a solid youngster who does a nice job checking nearly all the "responsible" boxes, but they still feel the need to micro-manage. Whether it's from needless suspicion or too much control, the parents are always looking over the trustworthy child's shoulder.

"Let me see your phone."

"What are you doing up in your room, hmm?"

"You need to try harder."

"You better not drive too fast because you know I track you."

The list of unwarranted orders goes on and on. It's almost as if these parents are trying to get their kid to not like them.

Again, most parents long to be good caregivers and influence their child to make good choices, but they discount how imperative it is to be strategic about when a necessary vs. unnecessary message is delivered. Why do some adults grapple with this? *Because I'm your parent, and you're just a clueless kid, and I can exercise my anxiety/arrogance and treat you however I want.* I keep restating this destructive doctrine because it's so difficult for many parents to overcome. The more I repeat it, the more terrible it sounds, especially since we now understand that great parenting cannot intermingle with this mindset.

The protection and development of a child are entrenched in most parents' minds, but as we've come to appreciate, Tri-C is about the correct way to fulfill these two commissions. The more you incorporate the Tri-C philosophy, the more inspired your kid becomes to act maturely and responsibly, which inspires you to trust your kid more, which inspires your kid to respect your parenting. It's a beautiful, perpetuating cycle that begins with you.

Yes, it is much easier to "tell" instead of allowing ourselves to loosen up a little, ask a rhetorical question, or engage in a considerate conversation. If we frivolously command, we assume our kid will robotically accept our demands and blindly obey out of respect. We don't want to have to explain or feel worried or potentially argue. Well, guess what? That's what we call disrespectful.

When this happens, the young "employee" on the receiving end of unnecessary dominance experiences negative feelings towards "the boss." An authoritarian approach indicates the parent does not trust the young human, who must primarily rely on the all-powerful overlord for either approval or instructions on making decisions. This sends the message, "You are not capable and cannot count on yourself to steer your life correctly." Or, "You're always doing something wrong." A kid who isn't allowed to navigate life to the proper degree is not allowed to build self-confidence adequately when the parent includes shame, guilt, inappropriate control, and manipulation.

> Parent: I guess a 93 on your test is okay, but why didn't you make a 100?
> Kid: I really studied, but some of the questions were hard.
> Parent: Apparently you didn't study enough. You're smarter than that.

> Parent: Why aren't you outside practicing? Why are you on your phone?
> Kid: Because Addy and I were selected for the eighth-grade pep rally committee, and we're talking about decorations.
> Parent: You should be hitting every day. I just bought you that net. Do you want to sit on the bench? Do you not want to be a good softball player?

(How about, "Okay, sweetie. Let me know when you're ready to go outside.")

As our child ages, we especially must train ourselves to be respectful and not intervene unless we absolutely have to. *I can "politely remind" my 13-year-old to put his napkin in his lap. I can "discuss" with my 15-year-old to consider changing her too short shorts before she leaves the house (which she will).*

Of course, we'll intercede if there's imminent danger or a disastrous mistake in the making, or if we recognize our child "isn't getting it," or unquestionably needs our mature guidance to achieve a goal/meet an expectation. Remember, a majority of healthy parenting involves nothing more than sitting back and allowing the kid to demonstrate which expectations will be met versus those that won't. In other words: *If you "get it" I'll leave you alone. But if you're not "getting it," then I'll jump in and see what the deal is, and we'll decide together what inevitably needs to be done so you can figure it out. I can interact respectfully because I'm in the business of you liking me, which incentivizes you to be receptive to my parenting. Oh yeah, I want to enjoy being around you, too!*

How about this:

Parent: Hey, have you been rehearsing your part?
Kid: Uh, no.
Parent: Isn't the audition next Monday?
Kid: Yes.
Parent: Are you still going for the lead?
Kid: Yes.
Parent: Okay, so what's the plan?
Kid: I guess I better start working on it.

The parent didn't "tell" the kid what to do, but did recognize that some guidance was needed. Just bringing up a subject in itself can be powerful enough. It can help the child take responsibility and address the situation effectively. But if no positive movement transpires, the parent can further investigate what's going on and appropriately help the kid connect the dots to achieve real success, which means real work has to be executed. Lean into then evaluate; repeat the process if needed.

When parents find themselves barking instructions and talking at their kid all the time, they are losing their child's respect and watering down their parenting. *The fewer words I have to use, the more meaningful they are, and the less I have to boss you. Show me you can be responsible, like putting your dishes in the dishwasher, regulating your screen time, practicing on your own, or doing your homework.* When we're incessantly and unnecessarily "instructing" our kid, we become like those people who post all the time on social media—their messages eventually lose meaning and we become increasingly annoyed.

Here's something else to consider: When you allow your child more independence and opportunities for the real world to teach life lessons, those experiences tend to be super powerful. *My job is to set you up for success, not guarantee your success.* We all learn many things the hard way because we're supposed to. Permit your child to learn some things the hard way, too. Nearly everything can be fixed.

A classic example is when parents are frustrated because they have to wake up their adolescent in time for school. This is an easy fix (much easier if you're a Connected Way parent because you've got credibility). Instead of submitting to our anxiety or enabling tendencies, we must execute an effective approach.

Why not try this: Parents tell the kid to use the alarm clock that has already been purchased, and Mom or Dad will not wake up "Sleeping Beauty" anymore. End of discussion. After the teen is late to school a few mornings and experiences everything that negatively brings, watch the magic happen as two significant elements transpire.

One, because internal motivation appears to be lacking, the parents are allowing external motivation (from school) for this adolescent to experience. Very powerful. Two, the kid will develop the skills to become self-responsible after the real-world consequences start mounting. This is called "the process." But for this to work, the parents must not demonstrate any temper when the teenager wakes up late and is frantic (or not), as they might conveniently be blamed.

Kid: I can't believe you didn't get me up!

Parent: Bahahaha... that's a good one. Have fun at school today!

If we can appropriately help a kid develop self-responsibility and have some laughs along the way (you can be funny and not sarcastic) instead of getting upset, that's a win.

Your household's trust-enriching culture also advances self-confidence and accountability, and the constant message of "how great you are" (but not false praise) and how much you love your kid adds to self-worth. Sometimes I'll treat families where the parents are misled in their thinking. Instead of enabling their kid, they're the opposite, and feel the best way to toughen up their child is to run the house military-style.

This approach makes it very difficult to create a connected relationship. Home is not boot camp, and the parent is not a drill sergeant. You're a devoted, responsible caregiver. Home is the safe haven of love, fun, stability, and respect. **Home is Sanctuary**. Your job is to lift that child up, not tear that child down. The world will do its best to pummel your kid; do not contribute to that garbage.

Up, up, up, always up! Never down and never criticize! No sarcasm, patronizing, or condescending words. Never ever. Promote self-confidence. Reinforce self-worth.

The better kids feel about themselves, the more they are willing to set goals, accept challenges, develop integrity, push themselves, take healthy risks, and feel empowered. In other words, when your children are confident, they will be more apt to put themselves out there and let society put them to the test. Your responsibility is to patch them up, encourage them, constructively coach them when necessary, and have their backs.

It's great hearing kids talk about how good they are at something—not in a cocky way, but in a way that demonstrates healthy self-pride. As parents, our job is to support that and not worry that our children are getting too big for their britches.

The more your kid is fueled to achieve (you supply the gas), the more that young human will engage in challenging endeavors. Do not fear—that will humble and toughen up your kid aplenty. There are tons of competitive opportunities for your bold child to experience, and your child's boldness is inexhaustibly fostered by—guess who?—*you*! Tri-C style! You know you're doing great as a parent when you randomly say to your kid, "You're awesome," and your child replies, "I know."

Complete

Regardless of the child's age, Tri-C is about executing parenting duties every day. And for some of you, you're in the home stretch and almost done raising that kid. As you complete your celebrated mission, the final few years look very different from any other child-rearing period.

This phase is easy to manage if your kid has reached late adolescence and you've been a Tri-C rock star. You are selfless and do not waver regarding expectations being met. You constantly stay relatable, advance self-worth, don't say things you don't mean, and promote dignity and self-responsibility. However, if your child is older and this is your initial exposure to this model, it is paramount for you to interact with the utmost respect, uphold the two primary parental tasks (protect and develop), and stay completely in charge.

Remember, you have all the authority. If your kid is a teenager, that should be clear. And if you've gotten this far in the book and there are still some arguments going on, let's do a brisk review.

I mentioned earlier that sometimes parents will return to my office because the power has somewhat shifted back to the kid(s). These parents have "permitted" their upper hand to deteriorate. Why? Because many children can be relentless in their quest to have certain things go their way. This is very normal. Parents then get tired of the challenges and allow themselves to become frustrated and either irritate the friction, and/or cave in. Thankfully, this is fixable.

I've said it before but let me say it again: Step one is to train yourself to not take the child seriously in disputes; therefore, you won't become incensed to any degree when your kid is being disagreeable or acting immature. This Tri-C fundamental must be mastered. Once this principle is embedded in your parenting, everything else can then tranquilly follow.

If your expectations and rules are reasonable and fair, **your child knows it and that is a fact.** When the kid is trying to push for something or start a quarrel about whatever it might be—to refresh—because you have learned to promptly activate yourself from interpersonal mode into the Tri-C business mode, the argument *never materializes*. Sooner than later, the child gives up and accepts your responsible verdict due to your staunchness, and can't justifiably be upset with you because you acted so respectfully during the brief interaction. This becomes the norm in these scenarios. Your mature, cool head and your consistency when it comes to addressing any potential discord rules. *Voila.*

I had a super nice dad and his tiresome 16-year-old son in my office. The father was trying to convince his adolescent to go to bed on school nights at a reasonable hour, as the snarky kid disrespectfully "tried" to convince the dad he should get to do what he wants. This apparently had been going on since the start of the school year, and it seemed the child had the advantage. What a beating.

As I listened to this, I thought *why is the dad putting up with this nonsense, and why is he still "asking" his son to get off his phone and go to sleep? And for that matter, why in the heck does this kid have his phone in his room on school nights, especially when he continues to demonstrate he cannot be responsible and go to bed at a decent hour?* (On school nights, phones/electronics should be turned in at least 15-30 minutes before bedtime, which applies to all kids until they graduate from high school—no exceptions. Again, lots of adults can't be responsible with their devices, so why should we expect kids to be? Do not fear; your child WILL adjust. By the way, this is a great representation of the healthy guardrails you provide.)

Once the father stepped out, I said, "Man, your dad sure is nice. Why doesn't he take your phone?"

"I dunno," he shrugged. "I guess he doesn't want me to get mad."

I responded, "So what if you do?"

The kid gave me a flat look, then slowly grinned, "I dunno."

Was the dad afraid of his son getting angry? Really? Paired with unrealistic expectations? As in, I trust (hope) you'll stop speeding if I'm a cop and keep asking you to slow down. But of course you won't slow down if I don't give you a ticket. Why would you?

On the other hand, I see parents who keep swinging the power saber throughout their child's upbringing to demonstrate dominance and try to force their kid to be more compliant. But once late adolescence arrives, a teen raised in that fashion is typically so disillusioned that the crucial parent-child relationship is in the trash. *I know I'm your kid, but you have no credibility. You never even tried to know me.*

You now understand how a majority of this parenting system works. If you've been an overly commanding parent, hopefully, it's not too late. And regarding the situation described above between the affable dad and his brooding son, my guess is, as you were reading, you might've already had in mind how you would properly handle it.

Probably something like this:

Dad: Well, son, we have a new policy on school nights that I'm going to strictly enforce so you can get enough sleep.
Kid: What's that supposed to mean?
Dad: You need at least eight hours, and because you have to

wake up at 6:30 in the morning, you have to turn in your phone by 10:00 at night.

Kid: Whoa, what?

Dad, whose delivery is so casual it feels like he's chatting with a friend about needing to change a sprinkler head: Yep. I should've done this a long time ago.

Kid: But I need it for homework! And I use it...for my alarm! And I listen to music on it so I can sleep!

Dad: No, you don't—and you have a laptop for school. We'll run by the store today and get you (another) alarm clock.

Kid, who feels his power starting to ooze out like a squashed bug: I can't believe you're actually going to take my phone. I'm almost 17 years old!

Dad doesn't say a word, maintains his statuesque posture, and simply gives his son the "I don't know what to tell you" look.

The kid knows he has zero leverage, yet understands this is a justifiable ruling, shakes his head, looks away, and scoffs, "Seriously. This is the dumbest thing ever."

The follow-up and unflinching application consists of the respectful dad never expressing emotion as he carries out this protocol every school night, compelling his son to accept this fair standard. Pushback inevitably ends. Victory. The authority is purely in the hands of the parent, and Dad exercises it productively. A sixteen-year-old has no more power over the parent than a six-year-old.

Vaping/Marijuana/Alcohol—The Big Three

However, when our kid goes from a six- to a sixteen-year-old, what a profound difference ten years can make. We all knew that one day our innocent child, who proudly held hands with us walking to elementary school, regularly crawled in our lap, excitedly ran everywhere, and let us wipe jelly off that sweet little face would eventually develop into a teenager. But if you had informed us that our precious child would evolve into some unrecognizable version of an intolerable adolescent who we continually caught vaping, or smoking marijuana, or drinking, we would've been horrified.

Which leads me to this. Experimentation is relatively normal and has been happening for a long time, so do not be shocked if you catch your kids trying something a time or two. Although a decent number of adolescents do not partake, when and if you do discover chemical mischievousness, there are meaningful implications in how that first "You're busted!" is handled.

Remember, we do not want to damage the relationship, we want to find out what's behind it, and we want to make sure the kid stops doing it. Within the conversation (not a sermon), state that you do not expect it to happen again. But sometimes, it does happen again.

A teenager tends to be curious, or maybe wants to be like an adult or feel accepted by some friends. Let's say you've got a good kid who does quite well at life, but you catch the child dabbling in high school. You do not detect any abuse or dependency—just a matter of your kid feeling peer pressure or being social/moronic/devious (which will still warrant a consequence).

Aside from being a strict rule follower, confidence and awareness are what keep an adolescent from thinking that smoking or drinking is acceptable. And coming from a rock-solid teen, it sounds something like this:

If I'm truly confident (not arrogant), I feel good about myself. I authentically feel good about myself because my folks are heavily invested in my well-being. I like them and they like me! They cultivate my strengths, support my dreams, and uncompromisingly provide me with the means to develop boldly. I do not have to give in to unhealthy ways to cope with life or falsely represent myself.

Although I'm just a teenager who believes I'm mostly bulletproof, I know drugs (including nicotine) and alcohol are bad for kids' brains and bodies; I do not want to disappoint my parents, nor do my close friends use (we are who our friends are, especially during high school). Also, I do not want illegal activities to compromise my future or derail the satisfying life I have established.

Okay, Brian, but what about a "good" kid from a "good" home who keeps trying to vape or use marijuana or drink alcohol? That unfortunate young human most likely wasn't doing as well as the parents had thought. And maybe the caregivers weren't quite as dialed in as they could've been. Aside from normal teenager-parent disconnect, some kids are skillful at disguising personal troubles and hiding contraband. Therefore, it's the adults' job to explore what's truly happening. "Why is my child doing bad things?"

Vaping: Kids who like to vape saw some peers do it and thought it looked neato. So they try it. It tastes good, they feel cool (yet initially conflicted), and they catch a quick nicotine buzz. Uh-oh. Nicotine is physiologically addictive. The more we do it, the more our cells crave it; now they think they need it.

But in the meantime, you're thinking: What's up with my kid who thought vaping was okay? As the parent who will not freak out, you can begin exploring by asking—you guessed it—"Why?" then objectively focus on the issue(s), whether it's curiosity, immaturity, peer pressure, or negative self-esteem and poor coping skills.

After briefly discussing (not lecturing) the dangers of vaping, and beginning the process of doing what's necessary to effectively address whatever the kid might be struggling with, you can initiate a one-week grounding from everything. The kid can go to school and do team-oriented activities (as you won't punish teammates), but other than that, there are zero privileges. This means no screens (including phone and television), no car, and no friends. Your child can read books and play with sticks in the backyard, but that's it.

If busted again, then it's a two-week grounding, followed by nicotine tests twice a week until you're convinced the usage has stopped. As the responsible parent, you can partner with your child to resolve the initial matter that persuaded said kid to vape. You can also execute reasonable consequences that will press your child to stop. A "good" kid (or any kid, for that matter) has no business sucking on a vape device.

Groundings can be hugely inconvenient for parents, but if we *lecture lecture lecture* or compromise these measures along the way, we roll out the red carpet for the dreaded Directive Way and/or intermittent reward. Remember, no cracks in the parenting wall, and the consequences that come with consistency will do the talking as you always keep your cool. We must not give up or cave in, and firmly maintain healthy regulations no matter what. Children cannot afford for us to shortchange our parenting. Our pronounced commitment is to our kids' well-being, period.

Be consistent. Don't get lazy. Keep your cool.

Marijuana: The CDC and the American Academy of Child and Adolescent Psychiatry report that adolescent cannabis use is higher (no pun intended) than ever. Close to half of all high school kids admit to having used marijuana. Although marijuana is widely accepted in many social circles and expanding in legalization, long-term use increases the risk of psychosis, early onset of Alzheimer's, and suicidal ideation according to recent studies.

Marijuana is best buddies with apathy and escape. When high, most people are not too interested in anything other than being high. And because marijuana is insidious and does not police itself like alcohol (it's tough to get away with being drunk), people can avoid reality and smoke almost every day if they choose. They can stay chill and go undetected as they meet minimal expectations at work or school, wake up the next day, experience no hangover, and do it all over again. Once marijuana sinks its cunning claws into many of its younger victims, dependency takes over, and productivity/life skills go in the dumpster.

As discussed previously, teenagers are in the business of developing their identities and natural coping mechanisms, which prepare them for adulthood when life gets more difficult. When irresponsible parents "tolerate" their kids getting high, they're not sufficiently providing the opportunity for their children's coping mechanisms to expand. I've had countless 19- to 22-year-olds in my office who finally realized their moderate to heavy pot use throughout their teenage years arrested their development, as the drug hijacked valuable opportunities to deal with life issues. Many are immature, insecure, and self-loathing, and realize that the majority of their friendships are not real. They see their functioning peers "miles ahead of them." They are left to battle a powerful emotional addiction that prevents them from experiencing normal and developmental pain that naturally motivates humans to strive.

People hate to feel any pain and will do what must be done to relieve it, either by escape or by implementation of change, also known as growth. Self-growth: good. Self-medication: bad.

I once worked with a dad of two non-using teenagers, and we were discussing the growing popularity of cannabis use. To paraphrase, he said, "There's only so much room at the top. If this new generation of kids thinks it's okay to smoke that marijuana all the time, shoot, too bad for them. That makes it all the easier for my kids to be successful." *Truer words were never spoken.*

Tri-C consequences you will execute if you catch your kid with weed include the "why" and hazards conversation, followed by a full-blown, two-week grounding of everything—and I mean everything. A kid can find solace in the smallest perks, like watching TV or taking a smartphone to school because "I need it." Your child does not need it. Get that kid a flip phone to use during school hours if you must communicate for a real reason.

If caught smoking again within a month or two, there might be a problem. Implement the two-week grounding, but now include random drug tests. It typically takes two to three weeks for marijuana to leave someone's system unless usage is heavy. If it is, then you're looking at up to six weeks to test clean. If the child continually cannot pass a drug test or you continue to detect usage, especially after you've tried to have productive conversations and made the kid's life absolutely dismal, then there most likely is an issue. Find a good therapist, or community advocacy center, or look into treatment programs.

Regardless of all the preposterous propaganda your adolescent will try to sell you, do not allow marijuana to become a player in your child's life. An emotionally fragile kid can be too immature and susceptible to avoid its nefarious seduction. It has no place, especially during this critical brain and life-skill development period.

Alcohol: I know parents who "sort of" let their older teens drink, but this is a slippery slope, and honestly, I do not have a universal answer. In some European countries, people are permitted to drink at a younger age. Is this a good thing? I'm not sure. Does it help older adolescents "learn" how to consume more responsibly? Research suggests mixed results. But it's prohibited in the U.S. for people under the age of 21 and comes with a high price tag if kids are caught consuming/possessing it.

If your kid develops a drinking habit, you will know it. Adults can't hide a drinking habit. You cannot allow it to continue. Alcoholism is real, and it's a horror show. If you catch your child drunk or with alcohol, do not freak out. Have a brief, strong talk, then enact the hardline, two-week sentence. If it happens again within six to twelve months, slap that kid with another two-week grounding. But if alcohol infractions continue to mount, you've lost control, or there's a bigger problem. It's time to exercise your full responsibility and seek outside help.

There certainly are solid kids who struggle with various teen difficulties and never turn to substances. Still, because marijuana, alcohol, and vape devices are so readily obtainable and common among today's youth, the door is more open today than ever. Therefore, as the parent, please recognize that an adolescent knows it is illegal and wrong to drink or smoke (or consume any drug), and if regular usage of any chemical is present, you'll need to A) understand why the kid feels motivated to consume it, and B) take action to address the issue. If your young human is simply being a normal yet dopey teenager trying to get away with something, then you can put the screws to that naive individual. In other words, "I won't be responsible for you after you move out and become an adult, but this ain't happening on my watch."

Stress

Be careful about how much strain your kid can handle, as too much stress is toxic to childhood development. Society is becoming more competitive every day, and kids are *feeling it*. Young people are getting pushed harder and harder, and as the world gets smaller, children are exposed to things that they aren't developed enough to process. This creates stress, confusion, troubled feelings, etc., that potentially infects both kids and their parents!

Because children aren't mature enough to safeguard themselves from certain elements, parents are responsible for providing the needed insulation. Simply put, the more invested we are in our children, the more we commit to honoring our parental responsibilities, which helps us keep our finger on the pulse of how our kids are experiencing life.

We must stay dialed in at all costs.

Stress comes from school, other kids, coaches, and, yes, parents. And let me remind you to be aware of all the things a kid can experience electronically. Although some of it is perfectly fine, a lot of it is not, and nearly any child can be poisoned. This is not the same world we grew up in.

And I'd be remiss not to mention the all-time favorite, pressure-inducing, overwhelming stress monster: Feeling accepted by peers. This can cripplingly strain a kid to no end, cause a young person to do mind-blowingly stupid things, and/or throw a child into a turbulent, self-deprecating tailspin. Genuine self-confidence counters this timeless plight, and as we now know, confidence has to be built; it doesn't just magically appear. Chapter Four: *Confident* tells us parents that we are responsible for beginning the confidence-building process, then appropriately partner with our kid to continually reinforce it.

Regardless of age, there is a somewhat elusive "life balance" to maintain, and your children will need your guidance to help achieve it throughout their upbringing, so check this out: People (our kids) can get markedly better by listening to themselves talk about what's personally causing them stress. It helps them process overwhelming thoughts, which allows them to more clearly see what they're dealing with and effectively address it.

Therefore, the better your relationship with your children, the more likely they'll feel comfortable confiding in you about what's happening, and the more you can help them. And they're open to your priceless guidance because you've worked diligently—Tri-C style—to make sure *they like and trust you*.

As clever and worldly as kids try to act, recognize they haven't been around the sun enough times to understand what's going on with multitudes of things. Whether you're an essential sounding board, the knowledgeable adult who can offer guidance, or the responsible parent constructively interceding, stay connected because you are more vital to your children's well-being than anything or anyone. Again, they have to deal with various life factors—either traditional or contemporary—that can be too much for them to handle on their own.

Now, what's frustrating for many parents is when they recognize their inactive kid is smart, athletic, or talented in the arts, but lacks initiative. This confounds parents, and I see this regularly in my office.

What's needed is some parental "leaning." But parents must be careful as they differentiate between leaning into someone and pushing someone. Pushing tends to backfire. No one likes to be pushed—not you; not me; and not your kid. Partnering, holding conversations (not speeches), and reinforcing a hard-working family protocol is the Tri-C way to recognize a child's strengths and grow them, not sabotage them.

To refresh, your child's strengths must be developed to build self-confidence and a healthy identity. Do not slack on this undertaking. Again, see what your kid is good at and provide the support to help advance that specific talent (e.g., private or group lessons, summer leagues/studios, community youth programs, regular participation in competitions/competitive leagues, etc.). However, if your kid happens to be more of a jack of all trades, you should see steady demonstrations of involvement in a number of different pursuits during childhood/adolescence.

Throughout the earlier years, most parents provide their children with a handful of different activities to experience, then see what sticks. What's different about today's society is that children are now lured away from developing their healthy opportunities because the electronic world is calling. It's got a powerful voice. It screams, *Hey kid! Get lost in me because I'm a lot more fun than rehearsing, studying, practicing, reading, going outside, interacting in-person, playing an instrument, or doing art.* Parents' former welcomed partner, boredom, is no longer a mainstay of wholesome prodding.

Now back to being pushy. Although sports and the arts are not exempt, the main area where we see parents go bananas is academics. As adults, we know—but sometimes disregard—that life mostly begins after college or after our mid-20s. Yes, earning a scholarship can help. Yes, it's more difficult these days to get into a stellar university, and yes, some initial employers are paying more attention to GPAs. But overall prosperity in life is determined by what we do after college or after we've been on our own for a while, not necessarily where we went to school, how long it took us to graduate, or what our GPA was.

Confidence, connections, and a strong work ethic will almost always get us where we want to go.

We also recognize that not every kid is designed to attend college. Although it certainly creates more opportunities, most of us know people who didn't step onto a college campus and built prosperous, fulfilling lives for themselves. Unless your child plans to do something spectacular like work for NASA, go to Harvard Medical School, be an investment banker on Wall Street, or play Division 1 college ball then advance to the pros, how critical is it for your kid to go to an "elite" college? For that matter, how many actual "bad" colleges are there?

It is important for our kid to understand the value of making good grades, but do we punish our middle- or high-schooler for not making straight A's? And do we radiate disappointment if our kid doesn't make the A team, first chair, go to Duke, or land the lead role? There's that old saying: *It's not the grades you make, it's the hands you shake.* The more confident your child is, the more that young adult feels comfortable networking and meeting valuable individuals.

Recognize, your teenager or tween is still just a kid. Relaxing and having *childhood* fun is a must because it's a wonderful luxury that will inevitably come to an end. So ask yourself: Am I appropriately partnering with my kid and/or appropriately leaning, or does my heavy determination to demandingly push my child stem from my own anxiety or personal desires?

Our job is to relieve our kid's stress, not create it.

Parenting is a long game, but life itself is a longer game, so what we do or do not during adolescence doesn't unequivocally define any of us. Often, our passions aren't discovered until sometime in adulthood, so try not to get bent on obsessing about your kid(s) not demonstrating a burning desire to pursue a certain undertaking—just make sure to religiously limit screen time and endorse meaningful activities.

Being a Tri-C parent, you strongly value the Connected Way relationship, which indicates you are committed to listening to your young human, honoring how your kid feels with conversations, finding the sweet spot of effective parenting by helping your child develop, and knowing who that person is.

Let's circle back to the enchantment of electronics. Here's what lots of parents say: "What stinks is that when my child does have free time, instead of spending it doing something worthwhile, my kid is staring at a device—ugh!" If that's the case and that young person is demonstrating the choice not to use free time more usefully, then *firmly* enact the screen time protocol of only a few hours on school days, and four to six hours a day on weekends (again, depending on age, occasion, and met expectations). Don't get suckered or become a pushover when your offspring tries to guilt or bully you about needing more time on devices because that's malarky. And if your child does become significantly involved in a substantial extracurricular, screen time will automatically minimize by default! Win-win!

Future

With some exceptions, there are five common options that can happen after high school graduation:

1. Go to a four-year university. If it's financed by the parents and the kid wants to continue that arrangement by making good grades, not getting pregnant or getting anyone pregnant, nor experiencing any scholastic or legal troubles, then parental funding can continue.

2. Go to a trade school. If it's local, recognize the parents' reasonable rules as an adult living in their house.

3. Go to a local community college, live at home, and recognize the parents' reasonable rules as an adult living in their house. Either attend full-time or get a part-time job and take a few classes each semester until a determination is made as to what's next.

4. Join the military.

5. Get a full-time job and move out sooner than later.

The end of adolescence tends to be a bittersweet time for parents. You've just spent 18 to 19 years being responsible for another human, and those days are coming to a close. If this is your only child or the last to leave, you become the empty nester and life becomes about you again (*I know—weird*). If you still have a few more ducks in waiting, you will miss the oldest duckling terribly upon departure.

If the military is beckoning, well, that phase of life is self-explanatory. If your kid is going to hang around for another year or two and work, attend community college, or go to trade school, then "partner up" to create fair house rules. And if the kid is leaving for a four-year college, hopefully you feel confident that all hurdles can be handled. But if you've got justifiable concerns because your older teen experienced or currently is experiencing some life difficulties, is going off to college right away the best idea?

College isn't going anywhere, but some parents think it's now or never. They say, "good luck," cross their fingers, and hope their unequipped young adult will be okay. But a kid fresh out of high school and leaving home needs to possess a certain mindset in order to experience success at a university:

I can be competent away from my parent(s). I am responsible enough and can figure out how to balance my time. I've got to prioritize academics, then socializing comes after that. I might occasionally feel somewhat unsettled because I'm a new college student, but that's okay. I think I know, or maybe I don't know, exactly what I want to do for a living after graduation; however, I recognize the value of a degree and possess the abilities to stay in school.

If your kid hits these maturity marks, the young academic should be in decent shape for independent college living. But what about the student who, somewhere along the way, does not adequately earn the right to continue to receive your financial support? I'm merely stating that if you feel your child "must" leave for college at all costs, and if your concerns regarding sustained success are valid, then be prepared for a possible early exit from campus, followed by a return home for a year or two, getting a job immediately (do not compromise on this), possibly taking some community college classes, and experiencing an important developmental phase in maturity.

If your kid is either slow to launch or needs to make a home pit stop, all is not lost. You can be the parent who appropriately supports this new adult who is in limbo and will figure it out sooner than later. You have more than likely groomed your child to know what needs to be done to eventually carve out a fulfilling life, whether a college degree is earned or not. We can sit in the boat and offer some directions, but everyone has to paddle their own canoe. Your child is now on the verge of becoming a grown-up and will soon enter the realm of total self-responsibility. So, no matter who or what your kid becomes or experiences along the way, your mission remains the same: to be the everlasting bedrock of proper support.

Well, mighty parent, I think that's it! I truly hope this was helpful. This model has been in the making for a long time, and I've been working on it for most of my professional career (*and at home!*). Again, do not be reluctant to reread certain sections, chapters, or the entire thing. As a matter of fact, I'm going to highly recommend it. It's like rewatching an involved movie—we catch so much more the second or third time through. And remember, if you find yourself getting flustered and wanting to resort to your old, unproductive ways, always go back to the timeless fundamentals.

Here are some of the main attractions:

1. Try to look at your child objectively and don't have unrealistic expectations for your mini-human. That individual is just a kid.

2. Some things are meant to be taken seriously; however, when a disagreement tries to emerge, do not take the kid seriously and get emotionally provoked. Nearly everything can be worked out with a respectful conversation. Try not to abandon respectfulness because it's a necessary pillar of positive relationships.

3. Prioritize what's best for your child over your potential selfishness or anxiety. Address your personal issues if

you must. Your kid needs you to be solid as an oak.

4. Earnestly ask "why" a rule was broken or an expectation was not met, then take it from there.

5. Do not argue. Maintain your composure as a dignified parent.

6. Do not shame, guilt, or criticize—your mission is to elevate your child's self-worth, not tear it apart.

7. Always uphold and reinforce reasonable expectations, and always try for a considerate delivery.

8. Try not to enable or over-control. *Empower.*

9. Be Connected, not Directive. Do what you must to foster a magnificent relationship as you consistently find the sweet spot of parenting. (Appropriate control combined with a great union.)

10. Try to be a complete parent every day, month, and year. And don't forget, kids are designed to have fun, so have fun with your kids!

What a job it is to be a parent. Your child needs you now and always, and Tri-C will always be here for you. *Follow the formula.*

Thanks again and God bless,
Brian

References

American Academy of Child and Adolescent Psychiatry. (2019, October) *Marijuana and Teens*, No. 106. https://www.aacap.org/AACAP/Families_and_Youth/Facts_for_Families/FFF-Guide/Marijuana-and-Teens-106.aspx

Britannica, T. Editors of Encyclopedia. (2020, May 5) *Stanford Prison Experiment*. Encyclopedia Britannica. https://www.britannica.com/event/Stanford-Prison-Experiment

Centers for Disease Control and Prevention. (2021, March 22) *Data and Statistics on Children's Mental Health*. https://www.cdc.gov/childrensmentalhealth/data.html

Centers for Disease Control and Prevention. (2017, April 13) *What You Need to Know About Marijuana Use in Teens*. https://www.cdc.gov/marijuana/factsheets/teens.htm

Cline, F. & Fay, F. (2006) *Parenting With Love and Logic*. Colorado Springs, CO: NavPress Publishing Group.

DeMille, C.B. (Director). (1956) *The Ten Commandments* [Film]. Cecil B. DeMille Productions.

Dobson, James C. (2004) *The New Strong-Willed Child*. IL: Tyndale.

Favreau, J. (Writer), & Filoni, D. (Director). (2019, November 11) Chapter 1: The Mandalorian (Season 1, Episode 1) [TV Series]. In J. Favreau, D. Filoni, K. Kennedy (Executive Producers), *The Mandalorian*. Lucasfilm, Fairview Entertainment, Golem Entertainment.

Heckerling, Amy (Director). (1982). *Fast Times at Ridgemont High* [Film]. Universal.

Kemp, Carla. (2018, November 5) *AAP recommends positive discipline rather than physical, verbal punishment*. AAP News. American Academy of Pediatrics. https://www.aappublications.org/news/2018/11/05/nce18discipline110518

King, Stephen. (2022) *Fairytale*. New York: Scribner.

Landreth, Garry L. (2002) *Play Therapy: The Art of the Relationship*. New York: Brunner-Routledge.

Mehrabian, Albert. (1972) *Nonverbal Communication*. United Kingdom: Taylor & Francis.

National Alliance on Mental Illness. (2017, December) *Anxiety Disorders*. https://www.nami.org/About-Mental-Illness/Mental-Health-Conditions/Anxiety-Disorders

National Alliance on Mental Health. (2018, July) *Anxiety Disorders*. https://www.nimh.nih.gov/health/topics/anxiety-disorders

Practical Psychology. (2020, April) *Havighurst's Developmental Task Theory*. https://practicalpie.com/havighursts-developmental-task-theory/

Scharf, Richard S. (2000) *Theories of Psychotherapy and Counseling*. Belmont, CA: Wadsworth.

Zeltser, Francyne. (2021, June 29) *Raising Successful Kids*. CNBC. https://www.cnbc.com/2021/06/29/child-psychologist-explains-4-types-of-parenting-and-how-to-tell-which-is-right-for-you.html

About The Author

Dr. Brian Rees is a native Texan and grew up in the Dallas/Fort Worth area. While obtaining his Master's & PhD at the University of North Texas, Dr. Rees managed a mental health clinic and instructed undergraduates and graduates in psychology and counseling courses. In 2007, he opened his private practice with a primary focus on therapy for tweens, adolescents, young adults, and their parents. After living the life of a lead singer in a rock band in his 20's, he is now trying to keep up with his wife and three daughters.

Dr. Rees is the founder of Tri-C Parenting. After spending close to 20 years counseling kids and their parents, he has created a fundamental and universally applicable system to parent constructively in today's and tomorrow's world.

Visit www.TriCParenting.com for more info.

If you enjoyed this book, please leave a review and help me reach more readers like you!

www.ingramcontent.com/pod-product-compliance
Lightning Source LLC
LaVergne TN
LVHW011911080426
835508LV00007BA/474